NIV개정

지혜의 성경 영어 잠언 따라쓰기 2

이 름 : ____________________

시작한 날 : ____________________

끝마친 날 : ____________________

또 어려서부터 성경을 알았나니 성경은 능히 너로 하여금 그리스도 예수 안에 있는 믿음으로 말미암아 구원에 이르는 지혜가 있게 하느니라
모든 성경은 하나님의 감동으로 된 것으로 교훈과 책망과 바르게 함과 의로 교육하기에 유익하니 이는 하나님의 사람으로 온전하게 하며 모든 선한 일을 행할 능력을 갖추게 하려 함이라

디모데후서 3장 15-17절

잠언의 소개

잠언은 '속담' 또는 '격언'이라는 뜻이며, 기록연대는 솔로몬의 재위기간인 B.C. 970-930년경으로 추정됩니다. 저자는 솔로몬(1:1), 아굴(30:1), 르무엘의 어머니(31:1), 지혜 있는 자(22:17)까지 포함하여 4명입니다.

잠언은 하나님의 백성이 갖추어야 할 지혜의 근본 내용과 옳고 그름을 판단하는 지혜의 본질에 대한 규명과 삶의 현장에서의 하나님의 백성으로 살아가는 구체적인 사례가 기록되어 있습니다.

영어 잠언 따라 쓰기의 특징

1. 영어 성경이 없어도 영어 성경을 읽고 쓰는 것이 즐겁습니다.
2. 영어 성경을 쓰면서 삶의 지혜가 자라납니다.
3. 영어 성경을 쓰면서 하나님의 자녀로 바르게 자라납니다.
4. 영어 성경을 쓰면서 옳고 그른 것을 판단하는 기준이 생겨납니다.
5. 영어 성경을 쓰면서 순종적인 자녀로 성장하게 됩니다.
6. 영어 성경을 쓰면서 좋은 글씨체를 갖게 됩니다.
7. 각 페이지마다 숙어와 예문, 각 장의 단어 뜻풀이를 통해 영어 해석에 도움이 됩니다.
8. 부록에 수록된 원어민 발음과 한글개역개정을 통해 영어 잠언이 쉽게 읽어집니다.

말씀을 따라 쓰기 전에 알아 두세요.

1. 말씀을 쓰기 전 성령님의 도움으로 영어 성경을 깨닫게 해 달라고 기도해 보세요.
2. 쓰면서 큰 소리로 따라 읽으세요. 암송의 효과를 얻을 수 있어요.
3. 모르는 단어는 함께 수록되어 있는 뜻을 찾아보세요.
   영어 성경을 쉽게 이해하게 해 줄 거예요.
4. 쓴 만큼의 날짜를 꼭 적어 보세요.
   얼마나 규칙적으로 영어 성경쓰기를 했는지 알 수 있습니다.
5. 영어 성경을 쓰고 난 후 부모님이나 선생님께 보여드려 검사를 받으세요.
   부모님과 선생님은 어린이에게 하고 싶은 말이나 축복의 문구를 써 주시면
   큰 힘이 됩니다.

Proverbs 16장 1~33절

1 To humans belong the plans of the heart, but from the LORD comes the proper answer of the tongue.

2 All a person's ways seem pure to them, but motives are weighed by the LORD.

3 Commit to the LORD whatever you do, and he will establish your plans.

4 The LORD works out everything to its proper end—even the wicked for a day of disaster.

5 The LORD detests all the proud of heart. Be sure of this: They will not go unpunished.

proud of …을 자랑으로 생각하는
She may well be proud of her son. 그녀가 아들을 자랑하는 것도 당연하다.

6 Through love and faithfulness sin is
atoned for; through the fear of the
LORD evil is avoided.
7 When the LORD takes pleasure in
anyone's way, he causes their ene-
mies to make peace with them.
8 Better a little with righteousness
than much gain with injustice.
9 In their hearts humans plan their
course, but the LORD establishes
their steps.
10 The lips of a king speak as an oracle,
and his mouth does not betray justice.
11 Honest scales and balances belong
to the LORD; all the weights in the
bag are of his making.

belong to …에 속하다
That house doesn't belong to me any more. 그 집은 더 이상 내 것이 아니야.

12 Kings detest wrongdoing, for a
throne is established through right-
eousness.
13 Kings take pleasure in honest lips;
they value the one who speaks what
is right.
14 A king's wrath is a messenger of
death, but the wise will appease it.
15 When a king's face brightens, it
means life; his favor is like a rain
cloud in spring.
16 How much better to get wisdom
than gold, to get insight rather than
silver!
17 The highway of the upright avoids
evil; those who guard their ways pre-

take pleasure in …을 즐기다
Everybody takes pleasure in eating. 누구나 음식 먹는 걸 즐긴다.

serve their lives.
18 Pride goes before destruction, a
haughty spirit before a fall.
19 Better to be lowly in spirit along
with the oppressed than to share
plunder with the proud.
20 Whoever gives heed to instruction
prospers, and blessed is the one
who trusts in the LORD.
21 The wise in heart are called discerni-
ng, and gracious words promote in-
struction.
22 Prudence is a fountain of life to the
prudent, but folly brings punish-
ment to fools.
23 The hearts of the wise make their

along with …와 함께
Please come along with me. 함께 가주세요.

mouths prudent, and their lips pro-
mote instruction.
24 Gracious words are a honeycomb,
sweet to the soul and healing to the
bones.
25 There is a way that appears to be
right, but in the end it leads to
death.
26 The appetite of laborers works for
them; their hunger drives them on.
27 A scoundrel plots evil, and on their
lips it is like a scorching fire.
28 A perverse person stirs up conflict,
and a gossip separates close friends.
29 A violent person entices their
neighbor and leads them down a

lead to …로 이어지다
Cold may lead to all kinds of illness. 감기는 만병의 근원이다.

path that is not good.

30 Whoever winks with their eye is
plotting perversity; whoever purses
their lips is bent on evil.

31 Gray hair is a crown of splendor; it
is attained in the way of righteous-
ness.

32 Better a patient person than a warr-
ior, one with self-control than one
who takes a city.

33 The lot is cast into the lap, but its
every decision is from the LORD.

Proverbs 17장 1~28절

1 Better a dry crust with peace and

be bent (on) 여념이 없다
Jake is bent on his study. Jake는 공부에 열중해 있다.

quiet than a house full of feasting,
with strife.

2 A prudent servant will rule over a
disgraceful son and will share the in-
heritance as one of the family.

3 The crucible for silver and the furnace
for gold, but the LORD tests the heart.

4 A wicked person listens to deceitful
lips; a liar pays attention to a destruc-
tive tongue.

5 Whoever mocks the poor shows
contempt for their Maker; whoever
gloats over disaster will not go un-
punished.

6 Children's children are a crown to
the aged, and parents are the pride

pay attention to …에 주목하다
She pays attention to every detail. 그녀는 매사에 빈틈이 없다.

of their children.
7 Eloquent lips are unsuited to a
godless fool–how much worse lying
lips to a ruler!
8 A bribe is seen as a charm by the
one who gives it; they think suc-
cess will come at every turn.
9 Whoever would foster love covers
over an offense, but whoever re-
peats the matter separates close
friends.
10 A rebuke impresses a discerning
person more than a hundred lashes
a fool.
11 Evildoers foster rebellion against
God; the messenger of death will be

unsuited to …에게 적합하지 않은
He is unsuited to academic work. 그는 학술 활동에 부적합하다.

sent against them.
12 Better to meet a bear robbed of her
cubs than a fool bent on folly.
13 Evil will never leave the house of
one who pays back evil for good.
14 Starting a quarrel is like breaching a
dam; so drop the matter before a
dispute breaks out.
15 Acquitting the guilty and condemni-
ng the innocent–the LORD detests
them both.
16 Why should fools have money in
hand to buy wisdom, when they are
not able to understand it?
17 A friend loves at all times, and a
brother is born for a time of adver-

break out 발발[발생]하다
He predicted when war would break out. 그는 전쟁이 언제 일어날 것인지 예언하였다.

sity.
18 One who has no sense shakes hands
in pledge and puts up security for a
neighbor.
19 Whoever loves a quarrel loves sin;
whoever builds a high gate invites
destruction.
20 One whose heart is corrupt does not
prosper; one whose tongue is per-
verse falls into trouble.
21 To have a fool for a child brings grief;
there is no joy for the parent of a god-
less fool.
22 A cheerful heart is good medicine,
but a crushed spirit dries up the
bones.

dry up 바싹 마르다[말라붙다]
When oceans dry up, they leave salts. 바닷물이 마르면 소금이 쌓이게 된다.

23 The wicked accept bribes in secret
to pervert the course of justice.
24 A discerning person keeps wisdom in
view, but a fool's eyes wander to the
ends of the earth.
25 A foolish son brings grief to his
father and bitterness to the mother
who bore him.
26 If imposing a fine on the innocent is
not good, surely to flog honest offi-
cials is not right.
27 The one who has knowledge uses
words with restraint, and whoever
has understanding is even-tem-
pered.
28 Even fools are thought wise if they

in secret 비밀리에[몰래]
The meeting was held in secret. 그 회의는 비밀리에 열렸다.

keep silent, and discerning if they
hold their tongues.

Proverbs 18장 1~24절

1 An unfriendly person pursues selfish
ends and against all sound judg-
ment starts quarrels.
2 Fools find no pleasure in understa-
nding but delight in airing their
own opinions.
3 When wickedness comes, so does
contempt, and with shame comes
reproach.
4 The words of the mouth are deep
waters, but the fountain of wisdom

pleasure in 좋아하다
What is your pleasure in this matter? 이 일에 대한 당신의 의향은 어떤가요?

is a rushing stream.
5 It is not good to be partial to the
wicked and so deprive the innocent
of justice.
6 The lips of fools bring them strife,
and their mouths invite a beating.
7 The mouths of fools are their undoi-
ng, and their lips are a snare to their
very lives.
8 The words of a gossip are like choice
morsels; they go down to the in-
most parts.
9 One who is slack in his work is brother
to one who destroys.
10 The name of the LORD is a fortified
tower; the righteous run to it and

go down to …로 내려가다
His fame will go down to posterity. 그의 명성은 후손 대대로 전해질 것이다.

are safe.
11 The wealth of the rich is their fortif-
ied city; they imagine it a wall too
high to scale.
12 Before a downfall the heart is
haughty, but humility comes be-
fore honor.
13 To answer before listening—that is
folly and shame.
14 The human spirit can endure in
sickness, but a crushed spirit who
can bear?
15 The heart of the discerning acq-
uires knowledge, for the ears of the
wise seek it out.
16 A gift opens the way and ushers the

seek out (특히 많은 노력을 기울여) …을 찾아내다
He tried to seek out a friend in the city. 그는 그 시가에서 친구를 찾아내려고 했었다.

giver into the presence of the great.
17 In a lawsuit the first to speak seems
right, until someone comes forward
and cross-examines.
18 Casting the lot settles disputes and
keeps strong opponents apart.
19 A brother wronged is more unyieldi-
ng than a fortified city; disputes are
like the barred gates of a citadel.
20 From the fruit of their mouth a pers-
on's stomach is filled; with the har-
vest of their lips they are satisfied.
21 The tongue has the power of life
and death, and those who love it
will eat its fruit.
22 He who finds a wife finds what is

come forward (도움 등을 주겠다고) 나서다
He was hesitant to come forward. 그는 앞으로 나서지 못하고 우물쭈물했다.

good and receives favor from the
LORD.
23 The poor plead for mercy, but the
rich answer harshly.
24 One who has unreliable friends soon
comes to ruin, but there is a friend
who sticks closer than a brother.

Proverbs 19장 1~29절

1 Better the poor whose walk is
blameless than a fool whose lips are
perverse.
2 Desire without knowledge is not
good—how much more will hasty
feet miss the way!

plead for …을 탄원[호소]하다
He didn't cry out or plead for mercy. 그는 울지도, 자비를 구하지도 않았다.

3 A person's own folly leads to their
ruin, yet their heart rages against
the LORD.
4 Wealth attracts many friends, but
even the closest friend of the poor
person deserts them.
5 A false witness will not go unpunish-
ed, and whoever pours out lies will
not go free.
6 Many curry favor with a ruler, and
everyone is the friend of one who
gives gifts.
7 The poor are shunned by all their
relatives—how much more do their
friends avoid them! Though the
poor pursue them with pleading,

pour out (보통 한동안 숨기고 있던 감정 · 말이) 쏟아져 나오다
Pour out words in a steady flow. 조금도 중단 없이 말이 나오다.

they are nowhere to be found.
8 The one who gets wisdom loves life;
the one who cherishes understand-
ing will soon prosper.
9 A false witness will not go unpun-
ished, and whoever pours out lies
will perish.
10 It is not fitting for a fool to live in
luxury–how much worse for a slave
to rule over princes!
11 A person's wisdom yields patience;
it is to one's glory to overlook an of-
fense.
12 A king's rage is like the roar of a lion,
but his favor is like dew on the grass.
13 A foolish child is a father's ruin, and

rule over …을 지배, 통치하다
The king ruled over the subjects with justice. 왕은 국민을 공정하게 통치했다.

a quarrelsome wife is like the con-
stant dripping of a leaky roof.
14 Houses and wealth are inherited
from parents, but a prudent wife is
from the LORD.
15 Laziness brings on deep sleep, and
the shiftless go hungry.
16 Whoever keeps commandments
keeps their life, but whoever shows
contempt for their ways will die.
17 Whoever is kind to the poor lends to
the LORD, and he will reward them
for what they have done.
18 Discipline your children, for in that
there is hope; do not be a willing
party to their death.

reward for …에 대해 보답하다
I'm not seeking a reward for doing this. 대가를 바라고 하는 일은 아니다.

19 A hot-tempered person must pay
the penalty; rescue them, and you
will have to do it again.
20 Listen to advice and accept discip-
line, and at the end you will be
counted among the wise.
21 Many are the plans in a person's heart,
but it is the LORD's purpose that pre-
vails.
22 What a person desires is unfailing
love; better to be poor than a liar.
23 The fear of the LORD leads to life;
then one rests content, untouched
by trouble.
24 A sluggard buries his hand in the dish;
he will not even bring it back to his

untouched by …에 의해 동요되지 않은
There wasn't a place untouched by her. 그녀의 손길이 미치지 않은 곳이 없었다.

mouth!
25 Flog a mocker, and the simple will
learn prudence; rebuke the discern-
ing, and they will gain knowledge.
26 Whoever robs their father and driv-
es out their mother is a child who
brings shame and disgrace.
27 Stop listening to instruction, my son,
and you will stray from the words of
knowledge.
28 A corrupt witness mocks at justice,
and the mouth of the wicked gulps
down evil.
29 Penalties are prepared for mockers,
and beatings for the backs of fools.

gulp down 한 입에 꿀꺽 집어삼키다
I made an effort to gulp down tears. 나는 애써 눈물을 삼켰다.

Proverbs 20장 1~30절

1 Wine is a mocker and beer a brawler;
whoever is led astray by them is not
wise.

2 A king's wrath strikes terror like the
roar of a lion; those who anger him
forfeit their lives.

3 It is to one's honor to avoid strife, but
every fool is quick to quarrel.

4 sluggards do not plow in season; so
at harvest time they look but find
nothing.

5 The purposes of a person's heart are
deep waters, but one who has in-
sight draws them out.

in season 제철인[한창인]
Strawberries are in season these days. 요즘은 딸기가 제철이다.

6 Many claim to have unfailing love,
but a faithful person who can find?
7 The righteous lead blameless lives;
blessed are their children after them.
8 When a king sits on his throne to
judge, he winnows out all evil with
his eyes.
9 Who can say, "I have kept my heart
pure; I am clean and without sin"?
10 Differing weights and differing
measures—the LORD detests them
both.
11 Even small children are known by
their actions, so is their conduct re-
ally pure and upright?
12 Ears that hear and eyes that see—

sit on …의 위에 있다
People sit on benches in the park. 사람들은 공원의 벤취에 앉는다.

the LORD has made them both.
13 Do not love sleep or you will grow
poor; stay awake and you will have
food to spare.
14 "It's no good, it's no good!" says the
buyer—then goes off and boasts
about the purchase.
15 Gold there is, and rubies in abund-
ance, but lips that speak knowl-
edge are a rare jewel.
16 Take the garment of one who puts
up security for a stranger; hold it in
pledge if it is done for an outsider.
17 Food gained by fraud tastes sweet,
but one ends up with a mouth full
of gravel.

end up with 결국 …하게 되다
What do you end up with? 결국 어떻게 했어?

18 Plans are established by seeking
advice; so if you wage war, obtain
guidance.
19 A gossip betrays a confidence; so
avoid anyone who talks too much.
20 If someone curses their father or
mother, their lamp will be snuffed
out in pitch darkness.
21 An inheritance claimed too soon will
not be blessed at the end.
22 Do not say, "I'll pay you back for this
wrong!" Wait for the LORD, and he
will avenge you.
23 The LORD detests differing weights,
and dishonest scales do not please
him.

snuff out …을 완전히 끝내다[파괴하다]
His goal was to snuff out the regime. 그의 목표는 그 제국의 멸망이었다.

24 A person's steps are directed by the
LORD. How then can anyone under-
stand their own way?
25 It is a trap to dedicate something
rashly and only later to consider one's
vows.
26 A wise king winnows out the wicked;
he drives the threshing wheel over
them.
27 The human spirit is the lamp of the
LORD that sheds light on one's in-
most being.
28 Love and faithfulness keep a king
safe; through love his throne is
made secure.
29 The glory of young men is their

be directed by …가 감독을 맡다
The movie was directed by Steven Spielberg. 그 영화는 스티븐 스필버그가 감독했다.

strength, gray hair the splendor of
the old.
30 Blows and wounds scrub away evil,
and beatings purge the inmost being.

Proverbs 21장 1~31절

1 In the LORD's hand the king's heart is
a stream of water that he channels
toward all who please him.
2 A person may think their own ways
are right, but the LORD weighs the
heart.
3 To do what is right and just is more
acceptable to the LORD than sacrifice.
4 Haughty eyes and a proud heart—

a stream of water 물줄기
The fire brigade played a stream of water on flames. 소방대가 불길에 물을 퍼부었다.

the unplowed field of the wicked
–produce sin.
5 The plans of the diligent lead to profit
as surely as haste leads to poverty.
6 A fortune made by a lying tongue is
a fleeting vapor and a deadly snare.
7 The violence of the wicked will drag
them away, for they refuse to do
what is right.
8 The way of the guilty is devious, but
the conduct of the innocent is up-
right.
9 Better to live on a corner of the roof
than share a house with a quarrel-
some wife.
10 The wicked crave evil; their neighb-

drag away [나무 따위]를 뽑아내다
The woodcutter dragged away a tree. 나무꾼은 나무를 뽑아냈다.

ors get no mercy from them.
11 When a mocker is punished, the
simple gain wisdom; by paying at-
tention to the wise they get knowl-
edge.
12 The Righteous One takes note of the
house of the wicked and brings the
wicked to ruin.
13 Whoever shuts their ears to the cry of
the poor will also cry out and not be
answered.
14 A gift given in secret soothes anger,
and a bribe concealed in the cloak
pacifies great wrath.
15 When justice is done, it brings joy to
the righteous but terror to evildoers.

take note of …에 주목[주의]하다, 알아채다
Take note of what he says. 그의 말에 주목 하세요.

16 Whoever strays from the path of
prudence comes to rest in the com-
pany of the dead.
17 Whoever loves pleasure will bec-
ome poor; whoever loves wine and
olive oil will never be rich.
18 The wicked become a ransom for the
righteous, and the unfaithful for the
upright.
19 Better to live in a desert than with a
quarrelsome and nagging wife.
20 The wise store up choice food and
olive oil, but fools gulp theirs down.
21 Whoever pursues righteousness and
love finds life, prosperity and honor.
22 One who is wise can go up against

stray from …에서 빗나가다
Do not stray from what I teach. 내가 가르친 것으로부터 벗어나지 마세요.

the city of the mighty and pull
down the stronghold in which they
trust.
23 Those who guard their mouths and
their tongues keep themselves from
calamity.
24 The proud and arrogant person–
"Mocker" is his name–behaves with
insolent fury.
25 The craving of a sluggard will be
the death of him, because his hands
refuse to work.
26 All day long he craves for more, but
the righteous give without sparing.
27 The sacrifice of the wicked is det-
estable–how much more so when

all day long 온종일
The wind whistled all day long. 바람이 하루 종일 휙휙 불었다.

brought with evil intent!

28 A false witness will perish, but a careful
listener will testify successfully.

29 The wicked put up a bold front, but
the upright give thought to their
ways.

30 There is no wisdom, no insight, no
plan that can succeed against the
LORD.

31 The horse is made ready for the day
of battle, but victory rests with the
LORD.

Proverbs 22장 1~29절

1 A good name is more desirable than

rest with …에 달려 있다
It rests with you to decide. 결정은 네게 달려 있다.

great riches; to be esteemed is bet-
ter than silver or gold.
2 Rich and poor have this in common:
The LORD is the Maker of them all.
3 The prudent see danger and take
refuge, but the simple keep going
and pay the penalty.
4 Humility is the fear of the LORD; its
wages are riches and honor and life.
5 In the paths of the wicked are snares
and pitfalls, but those who would
preserve their life stay far from them.
6 Start children off on the way they
should go, and even when they are
old they will not turn from it.
7 The rich rule over the poor, and the

be esteemed 존대 받다
She was esteemed the perfect novelist. 그녀는 완벽한 소설가로 여겨졌다.

borrower is slave to the lender.
8 Whoever sows injustice reaps
calamity, and the rod they wield in
fury will be broken.
9 The generous will themselves be
blessed, for they share their food
with the poor.
10 Drive out the mocker, and out goes
strife; quarrels and insults are ended.
11 One who loves a pure heart and
who speaks with grace will have the
king for a friend.
12 The eyes of the LORD keep watch
over knowledge, but he frustrates
the words of the unfaithful.
13 The sluggard says, "There's a lion

keep (a) watch over …을 지키다, 감시하다
Always keep a good watch over the kids. 항상 아이들을 지켜보세요.

outside! I'll be killed in the public
square!"
14 The mouth of an adulteress woman
is a deep pit; a man who is under the
LORD's wrath falls into it.
15 Folly is bound up in the heart of a
child, but the rod of discipline will
drive it far away.
16 One who oppresses the poor to inc-
rease his wealth and one who gives
gifts to the rich—both come to
poverty.
17 Pay attention and turn your ear to
the sayings of the wise; apply your
heart to what I teach,
18 for it is pleasing when you keep

apply to …에 적용되다
They do not apply to schedules. 일람표에는 적용되지 않습니다.

them in your heart and have all of
them ready on your lips.
19 So that your trust may be in the
LORD, I teach you today, even you.
20 Have I not written thirty sayings for
you, sayings of counsel and knowl-
edge,
21 teaching you to be honest and to
speak the truth, so that you bring
back truthful reports to those you
serve?
22 Do not exploit the poor because
they are poor and do not crush the
needy in court,
23 for the LORD will take up their case
and will exact life for life.

take up (특히 이미 끝난 데서 시작하여) 계속하다
They didn't take up that issue at the meeting. 그들은 회의에서 그 문제를 거론하지 않았다.

24 Do not make friends with a hot-
tempered person, do not associate
with one easily angered,
25 or you may learn their ways and get
yourself ensnared.
26 Do not be one who shakes hands in
pledge or puts up security for debts;
27 if you lack the means to pay, your
very bed will be snatched from
under you.
28 Do not move an ancient boundary
stone set up by your ancestors.
29 Do you see someone skilled in their
work? They will serve before kings;
they will not serve before officials
of low rank.

associate with …와 어울리다
I don't care to associate with them. 나는 그 사람들과 교제하고 싶지 않다.

Proverbs 23장 1~35절

1 When you sit to dine with a ruler,
note well what is before you,
2 and put a knife to your throat if you
are given to gluttony.
3 Do not crave his delicacies, for that
food is deceptive.
4 Do not wear yourself out to get rich;
do not trust your own cleverness.
5 Cast but a glance at riches, and they
are gone, for they will surely sprout
wings and fly off to the sky like an
eagle.
6 Do not eat the food of a begru-
dging host, do not crave his delica-

wear yourself out …를 지치게[기진맥진하게] 만들다
The kids have totally worn me out. 아이들 때문에 난 완전히 기진맥진이다.

cies;
7 for he is the kind of person who is
always thinking about the cost. "Eat
and drink," he says to you, but his
heart is not with you.
8 You will vomit up the little you have
eaten and will have wasted your
compliments.
9 Do not speak to fools, for they will
scorn your prudent words.
10 Do not move an ancient boundary
stone or encroach on the fields of
the fatherless,
11 for their Defender is strong; he will
take up their case against you.
12 Apply your heart to instruction and

encroach on …을 침입하다
They encroach on your life. 그들이 너의 삶을 침해한다.

your ears to words of knowledge.
13 Do not withhold discipline from a
child; if you punish them with the
rod, they will not die.
14 Punish them with the rod and save
them from death.
15 My son, if your heart is wise, then
my heart will be glad indeed;
16 my inmost being will rejoice when
your lips speak what is right.
17 Do not let your heart envy sinners,
but always be zealous for the fear of
the LORD.
18 There is surely a future hope for you,
and your hope will not be cut off.
19 Listen, my son, and be wise, and set

cut off …을 자르다
Radio communication was abruptly cut off. 갑자기 통신이 두절되었다.

your heart on the right path:
20 Do not join those who drink too
much wine or gorge themselves on
meat,
21 for drunkards and gluttons become
poor, and drowsiness clothes them
in rags.
22 Listen to your father, who gave you
life, and do not despise your mother
when she is old.
23 Buy the truth and do not sell it—
wisdom, instruction and insight as
well.
24 The father of a righteous child has
great joy; a man who fathers a wise
son rejoices in him.

as well 또한, 역시
Do you love singing as well? 노래 부르는 것도 좋아하십니까?

25 May your father and mother rejoice;
may she who gave you birth be joy-
ful!
26 My son, give me your heart and let
your eyes delight in my ways,
27 for an adulterous woman is a deep
pit, and a wayward wife is a nar-
row well.
28 Like a bandit she lies in wait and
multiplies the unfaithful among men.
29 Who has woe? Who has sorrow?
Who has strife? Who has com-
plaints? Who has needless bruises?
Who has bloodshot eyes?
30 Those who linger over wine, who go
to sample bowls of mixed wine.

linger over …을 두고 미적거리며 시간을 끌다
Do not linger too long over your books. 우물쭈물 책을 읽지 말라.

31 Do not gaze at wine when it is red,
when it sparkles in the cup, when it
goes down smoothly!
32 In the end it bites like a snake and
poisons like a viper.
33 Your eyes will see strange sights,
and your mind will imagine confus-
ing things.
34 You will be like one sleeping on the
high seas, lying on top of the rig-
ging.
35 "They hit me," you will say, "but I'm
not hurt! They beat me, but I don't
feel it! When will I wake up so I can
find another drink?"

sleep on …을 하룻밤 자며 생각하다
Let me sleep on the plan. 하룻밤 자면서 그 계획을 잘 생각해볼게요.

Proverbs 24장 1~34절

1 Do not envy the wicked, do not desire
their company;
2 for their hearts plot violence, and
their lips talk about making trouble.
3 By wisdom a house is built, and
through understanding it is estab-
lished;
4 through knowledge its rooms are
filled with rare and beautiful trea-
sures.
5 The wise prevail through great power,
and those who have knowledge
muster their strength.
6 Surely you need guidance to wage

talk about …에 대해 이야기하다
Let's talk about your problem in plain terms. 솔직하게 너의 문제에 대해 얘기해보자.

war, and victory is won through
many advisers.
7 Wisdom is too high for fools; in the
assembly at the gate they must not
open their mouths.
8 Whoever plots evil will be known as
a schemer.
9 The schemes of folly are sin, and
people detest a mocker.
10 If you falter in a time of trouble, how
small is your strength!
11 Rescue those being led away to
death; hold back those staggering
toward slaughter.
12 If you say, "But we knew nothing
about this," does not he who weighs

lead away …을 데리고[끌고] 가다
The kidnapper led my child away! 저 유괴범이 내 아이를 데려갔어요!

the heart perceive it? Does not he
who guards your life know it? Will he
not repay everyone according to
what they have done?
13 Eat honey, my son, for it is good;
honey from the comb is sweet to
your taste.
14 Know also that wisdom is like honey
for you: If you find it, there is a future
hope for you, and your hope will not
be cut off.
15 Do not lurk like a thief near the
house of the righteous, do not plun-
der their dwelling place;
16 for though the righteous fall seven
times, they rise again, but the wicked

according to …에 의하면
Just do it according to the plan. 계획에 따라서만 행동해라.

stumble when calamity strikes.
17 Do not gloat when your enemy falls;
when they stumble, do not let your
heart rejoice,
18 or the LORD will see and disapprove
and turn his wrath away from them.
19 Do not fret because of evildoers or
be envious of the wicked,
20 for the evildoer has no future hope,
and the lamp of the wicked will be
snuffed out.
21 Fear the LORD and the king, my son,
and do not join with rebellious
officials,
22 for those two will send sudden
destruction on them, and who knows

send on …에 보내다
They send robots on long trips. 그들은 로봇을 장거리 여행에 보낸다.

what calamities they can bring?
23 These also are sayings of the wise:
To show partiality in judging is not
good:
24 Whoever says to the guilty, "You are
innocent," will be cursed by peo-
ples and denounced by nations.
25 But it will go well with those who
convict the guilty, and rich bless-
ing will come on them.
26 An honest answer is like a kiss on
the lips.
27 Put your outdoor work in order and
get your fields ready; after that,
build your house.
28 Do not testify against your neighbor

testify against …에게 불리한 증언을 하다
She refused to testify against her husband. 그녀는 남편에게 불리한 증언을 하기를 거부했다.

without cause–would you use your
lips to mislead?
29 Do not say, "I'll do to them as they
have done to me; I'll pay them back
for what they did."
30 I went past the field of the sluggard,
past the vineyard of someone who
has no sense;
31 thorns had come up everywhere,
the ground was covered with
weeds, and the stone wall was in
ruins.
32 I applied my heart to what I obs-
erved and learned a lesson from
what I saw:
33 A little sleep, a little slumber, a little

pay back for …에 대한 대금을 갚다
Some day I'll pay you back for this! 이것을 언젠가는 네게 갚아 주겠어!

folding of the hands to rest–
34 and poverty will come on you like a
thief and scarcity like an armed man.

Proverbs 25장 1~28절

1 These are more proverbs of Solomon,
compiled by the men of Hezekiah
king of Judah:
2 It is the glory of God to conceal a
matter; to search out a matter is the
glory of kings.
3 As the heavens are high and the earth
is deep, so the hearts of kings are
unsearchable.
4 Remove the dross from the silver,

search out …을 끝까지 찾아내다
Search out right over there. 바로 거기를 찾아보세요.

and a silversmith can produce a
vessel;
5 remove wicked officials from the
king's presence, and his throne will
be established through righteous-
ness.
6 Do not exalt yourself in the king's
presence, and do not claim a place
among his great men;
7 it is better for him to say to you,
"Come up here," than for him to hu-
miliate you before his nobles. What
you have seen with your eyes
8 do not bring hastily to court, for
what will you do in the end if your
neighbor puts you to shame?

put to shame (훨씬 뛰어나서) …을 부끄럽게 하다
Your praises put me to shame. 칭찬해 주시니 도리어 부끄럽다.

9 If you take your neighbor to court,
do not betray another's confidence,
10 or the one who hears it may shame
you and the charge against you will
stand.
11 Like apples of gold in settings of
silver is a ruling rightly given.
12 Like an earring of gold or an ornam-
ent of fine gold is the rebuke of a
wise judge to a listening ear.
13 Like a snow-cooled drink at harvest
time is a trustworthy messenger to
the one who sends him; he re-
freshes the spirit of his master.
14 Like clouds and wind without rain is
one who boasts of gifts never given.

boast of …을 뽐내다, 자랑하다
He boasts of being rich. 그는 부자라고 자랑한다.

15 Through patience a ruler can be
persuaded, and a gentle tongue
can break a bone.
16 If you find honey, eat just enough—
too much of it, and you will vomit.
17 Seldom set foot in your neighbor's
house—too much of you, and they
will hate you.
18 Like a club or a sword or a sharp
arrow is one who gives false
testimony against a neighbor.
19 Like a broken tooth or a lame foot
is reliance on the unfaithful in a time
of trouble.
20 Like one who takes away a garm-
ent on a cold day, or like vinegar

set foot in …에 발을 들여놓다
Do not set foot in my house again. 다시는 우리 집에 발을 들여놓지 마라.

poured on a wound, is one who sings
songs to a heavy heart.
21 If your enemy is hungry, give him
food to eat; if he is thirsty, give him
water to drink.
22 In doing this, you will heap burning
coals on his head, and the LORD
will reward you.
23 Like a north wind that brings unexp-
ected rain is a sly tongue—which
provokes a horrified look.
24 Better to live on a corner of the roof
than share a house with a quarrel-
some wife.
25 Like cold water to a weary soul is
good news from a distant land.

live on 계속 살다[존재하다]
He has enough money to live on. 그는 먹고 살만한 충분한 돈이 있다.

26 Like a muddied spring or a polluted
well are the righteous who give
way to the wicked.
27 It is not good to eat too much
honey, nor is it honorable to search
out matters that are too deep.
28 Like a city whose walls are broken
through is a person who lacks self-
control.

Proverbs 26장 1~28절

1 Like snow in summer or rain in
harvest, honor is not fitting for a fool.
2 Like a fluttering sparrow or a darting
swallow, an undeserved curse does

give way to …에 굽히다
Don't give way to such gloomy thoughts. 그런 우울한 생각들에 굴복하지 말아요.

not come to rest.
3 A whip for the horse, a bridle for the
donkey, and a rod for the backs of
fools!
4 Do not answer a fool according to his
folly, or you yourself will be just like
him.
5 Answer a fool according to his folly,
or he will be wise in his own eyes.
6 Sending a message by the hands of
a fool is like cutting off one's feet or
drinking poison.
7 Like the useless legs of one who is
lame is a proverb in the mouth of a
fool.
8 Like tying a stone in a sling is the

in a sling 삼각건으로
He had his arm in a sling. 그는 팔에 팔걸이 붕대를 하고 있었다.

giving of honor to a fool.
9 Like a thornbush in a drunkard's
hand is a proverb in the mouth of a
fool.
10 Like an archer who wounds at rand-
om is one who hires a fool or any
passer-by.
11 As a dog returns to its vomit, so
fools repeat their folly.
12 Do you see a person wise in their
own eyes? There is more hope for a
fool than for them.
13 A sluggard says, "There's a lion in
the road, a fierce lion roaming the
streets!"
14 As a door turns on its hinges, so a

in the mouth of …의 말에 의하면
The meeting is postponed in the mouth of James. 제임스 말에 의하면 그 미팅은 연기되었다.

sluggard turns on his bed.
15 A sluggard buries his hand in the
dish; he is too lazy to bring it back to
his mouth.
16 A sluggard is wiser in his own eyes
than seven people who answer
discreetly.
17 Like one who grabs a stray dog by
the ears is someone who rushes into
a quarrel not their own.
18 Like a maniac shooting flaming
arrows of death
19 is one who deceives their neighbor
and says, "I was only joking!"
20 Without wood a fire goes out; witho-
ut a gossip a quarrel dies down.

a fire goes out 불이 꺼지다
Don't let the fire go out. 불이 안 꺼지게 해요.

21 As charcoal to embers and as wood
to fire, so is a quarrelsome person
for kindling strife.
22 The words of a gossip are like choice
morsels; they go down to the in-
most parts.
23 Like a coating of silver dross on
earthenware are fervent lips with
an evil heart.
24 Enemies disguise themselves with
their lips, but in their hearts they
harbor deceit.
25 Though their speech is charming,
do not believe them, for seven
abominations fill their hearts.
26 Their malice may be concealed by

earthenware 도기의
The ttukbaegi is a kind of earthenware bowl. 뚝배기는 도기로 된 사발의 일종이다.

deception, but their wickedness will
be exposed in the assembly.
27 Whoever digs a pit will fall into it; if
someone rolls a stone, it will roll
back on them.
28 A lying tongue hates those it hurts,
and a flattering mouth works ruin.

Proverbs 27장 1~27절

1 Do not boast about tomorrow, for
you do not know what a day may
bring.
2 Let someone else praise you, and
not your own mouth; an outsider,
and not your own lips.

dig a pit 구덩이를 파다
He who digs a pit for others into it himself. 남을 빠뜨릴 구멍에 자신도 빠진다.

3 Stone is heavy and sand a burden,
but a fool's provocation is heavier
than both.
4 Anger is cruel and fury overwhe-
lming, but who can stand before
jealousy?
5 Better is open rebuke than hidden
love.
6 Wounds from a friend can be trusted,
but an enemy multiplies kisses.
7 One who is full loathes honey from
the comb, but to the hungry even
what is bitter tastes sweet.
8 Like a bird that flees its nest is anyone
who flees from home.
9 Perfume and incense bring joy to

flee from …에서 달아나다
The man is fleeing from the zoo. 남자가 동물원에서 도망치고 있다.

the heart, and the pleasantness of a
friend springs from their heartfelt
advice.
10 Do not forsake your friend or a friend
of your family, and do not go to
your relative's house when disaster
strikes you—better a neighbor nearby
than a relative far away.
11 Be wise, my son, and bring joy to my
heart; then I can answer anyone
who treats me with contempt.
12 The prudent see danger and take
refuge, but the simple keep going
and pay the penalty.
13 Take the garment of one who puts
up security for a stranger; hold it in

treat with …로 대하다
I do not treat with those as weak as you. 너 같은 약골은 상대하지 않는다.

pledge if it is done for an outsider.
14 If anyone loudly blesses their
neighbor early in the morning, it will
be taken as a curse.
15 A quarrelsome wife is like the dripp-
ing of a leaky roof in a rainstorm;
16 restraining her is like restraining the
wind or grasping oil with the hand.
17 As iron sharpens iron, so one person
sharpens another.
18 The one who guards a fig tree will eat
its fruit, and whoever protects their
master will be honored.
19 As water reflects the face, so one's
life reflects the heart.
20 Death and Destruction are never

like the wind 바람같이[아주 빨리]
That horse ran like the wind. 저 말은 바람처럼 빨랐다.

satisfied, and neither are human eyes.
21 The crucible for silver and the furn-
ace for gold, but people are tested
by their praise.
22 Though you grind a fool in a mortar,
grinding them like grain with a pes-
tle, you will not remove their folly
from them.
23 Be sure you know the condition of
your flocks, give careful attention to
your herds;
24 for riches do not endure forever,
and a crown is not secure for all gen-
erations.
25 When the hay is removed and new
growth appears and the grass from

secure for …를 위해 확보하다
This is a secure receipt for the mail you sent. 보낸 메일에 대한 보안 확인 메일입니다.

the hills is gathered in,
26 the lambs will provide you with
clothing, and the goats with the
price of a field.
27 You will have plenty of goats' milk
to feed your family and to nourish
your female servants.

Proverbs 28장 1~28절

1 The wicked flee though no one
pursues, but the righteous are as
bold as a lion.
2 When a country is rebellious, it has
many rulers, but a ruler with discern-
ment and knowledge maintains

provide with …을 공급하다[주다]
He can provide them with a lot of food. 그는 그들에게 많은 식량을 공급할 수 있다.

order.
3 A ruler who oppresses the poor is
like a driving rain that leaves no crops.
4 Those who forsake instruction praise
the wicked, but those who heed it
resist them.
5 Evildoers do not understand what is
right, but those who seek the LORD
understand it fully.
6 Better the poor whose walk is
blameless than the rich whose ways
are perverse.
7 A discerning son heeds instruction,
but a companion of gluttons dis-
graces his father.
8 Whoever increases wealth by talking

increase by …(만큼) 증가하다[늘리다]
The gravity will increase day by day. 중력은 날을 거듭할수록 증가할 것이다.

interest or profit from the poor
amasses it for another, who will be
kind to the poor.
9 If anyone turns a deaf ear to my
instruction, even their prayers are
detestable.
10 Whoever leads the upright along an
evil path will fall into their own trap,
but the blameless will receive a good
inheritance.
11 The rich are wise in their own eyes;
one who is poor and discerning
sees how deluded they are.
12 When the righteous triumph, there is
great elation; but when the wicked
rise to power, people go into hiding.

turn a deaf ear to …에 귀를 기울이지 않다
He turned a deaf ear to the rumours. 그는 그 소문들을 귀담아듣지 않았다.

13 Whoever conceals their sins does
not prosper, but the one who con-
fesses and renounces them finds
mercy.
14 Blessed is the one who always
trembles before God, but whoever
hardens their heart falls into
trouble.
15 Like a roaring lion or a charging
bear is a wicked ruler over a help-
less people.
16 A tyrannical ruler practices extort-
ion, but one who hates ill-gotten
gain will enjoy a long reign.
17 Anyone tormented by the guilt of
murder will seek refuge in the grave;

seek refuge 피신, 도피하다
Visitors may want to seek refuge somewhere. 이방인들은 어딘가에 피난처를 찾고 싶어 한다.

let no one hold them back.
18 The one whose walk is blameless is
kept safe, but the one whose ways
are perverse will fall into the pit.
19 Those who work their land will
have abundant food, but those
who chase fantasies will have their
fill of poverty.
20 A faithful person will be richly blessed,
but one eager to get rich will not
go unpunished.
21 To show partiality is not good—yet a
person will do wrong for a piece of
bread.
22 The stingy are eager to get rich and
are unaware that poverty awaits them.

be eager to …을 하고 싶어하다
We are eager to hear the outcome. 우리는 결과를 간절히 듣고 싶어한다.

23 Whoever rebukes a person will in
the end gain favor rather than one
who has a flattering tongue.
24 Whoever robs their father or mother
and says, "It's not wrong," is partner
to one who destroys.
25 The greedy stir up conflict, but
those who trust in the LORD will
prosper.
26 Those who trust in themselves are
fools, but those who walk in wis-
dom are kept safe.
27 Those who give to the poor will lack
nothing, but those who close their
eyes to them receive many curses.
28 When the wicked rise to power,

rather than …보다는
Seek the positive rather than the negative. 부정적인 것보다 긍정적인 것을 찾아라.

people go into hiding; but when the
wicked perish, the righteous thrive.

Proverbs 29장 1~27절

1 Whoever remains stiff-necked after
many rebukes will suddenly be de-
stroyed—without remedy.
2 When the righteous thrive, the
people rejoice; when the wicked
rule, the people groan.
3 A man who loves wisdom brings joy
to his father, but a companion of
prostitutes squanders his wealth.
4 By justice a king gives a country
stability, but those who are greedy

stiff-necked 목이 뻣뻣한(거만하고 고집 센)
He rejected me with stiff neck. 그는 나를 완고하게 거절했다.

for bribes tear it down.
5 Those who flatter their neighbors
are spreading nets for their feet.
6 Evildoers are snared by their own sin,
but the righteous shout for joy and
are glad.
7 The righteous care about justice for
the poor, but the wicked have no
such concern.
8 Mockers stir up a city, but the wise
turn away anger.
9 If a wise person goes to court with a
fool, the fool rages and scoffs, and
there is no peace.
10 The bloodthirsty hate a person
of integrity and seek to kill the

go to court 소송을 제기하다
I have to go to court today. 오늘 법원에 가봐야 해.

upright.
11 Fools give full vent to their rage,
but the wise bring calm in the end.
12 If a ruler listens to lies, all his officials
become wicked.
13 The poor and the oppressor have
this in common: The LORD gives
sight to the eyes of both.
14 If a king judges the poor with fairn-
ess, his throne will be established
forever.
15 A rod and a reprimand impart wisd-
om, but a child left undisciplined dis-
graces its mother.
16 When the wicked thrive, so does sin,
but the righteous will see their

give vent to (노여움 따위)를 터뜨리다, …을 발산시키다
She gave vent to her anger and jealousy. 그녀는 노여움과 질투심을 발산했다.

downfall.
17 Discipline your children, and they
will give you peace; they will bring
you the delights you desire.
18 Where there is no revelation, peop-
le cast off restraint; but blessed is
the one who heeds wisdom's in-
struction.
19 Servants cannot be corrected by
mere words; though they under-
stand, they will not respond.
20 Do you see someone who speaks
in haste? There is more hope for a
fool than for them.
21 A servant pampered from youth will
turn out to be insolent.

turn out 모습을 드러내다[나타나다]
How did the result turn out? 어떻게 결과가 나왔니?

22 An angry person stirs up conflict,
and a hot-tempered person com-
mits many sins.
23 Pride brings a person low, but the
lowly in spirit gain honor.
24 The accomplices of thieves are
their own enemies; they are put
under oath and dare not testify.
25 Fear of man will prove to be a
snare, but whoever trusts in the
LORD is kept safe.
26 Many seek an audience with a ruler,
but it is from the LORD that one
gets justice.
27 The righteous detest the dishonest;
the wicked detest the upright.

put under oath …를 맹세시키다
I think she should be put under oath. 나는 그녀가 선서를 해야 한다고 생각한다.

Proverbs 30장 1~33절

1 The sayings of Agur son of Jakeh—an
inspired utterance. This man's utter-
ance to Ithiel: "I am weary, God,
but I can prevail.
2 Surely I am only a brute, not a man;
I do not have human understanding.
3 I have not learned wisdom, nor have
I attained to the knowledge of the
Holy One.
4 Who has gone up to heaven and
come down? Whose hands have
gathered up the wind? Who has
wrapped up the waters in a cloak?
Who has established all the ends of

go up to …으로 (가까이) 가다
We had to go up to the roof. 우리는 옥상으로 올라갔습니다.

the earth? What is his name, and
what is the name of his son? Surely
you know!
5 "Every word of God is flawless; he is
a shield to those who take refuge in
him.
6 Do not add to his words, or he will
rebuke you and prove you a liar.
7 "Two things I ask of you, LORD; do
not refuse me before I die:
8 Keep falsehood and lies far from me;
give me neither poverty nor riches,
but give me only my daily bread.
9 Otherwise, I may have too much
and disown you and say, 'Who is
the LORD?' Or I may become poor

take refuge in …에 피난하다
They took refuge in the embassy compound. 그들은 대사관으로 피신했다.

and steal, and so dishonor the name
of my God.
10 "Do not slander a servant to their
master, or they will curse you, and
you will pay for it.
11 "There are those who curse their
fathers and do not bless their
mothers;
12 those who are pure in their own
eyes and yet are not cleansed of
their filth;
13 those whose eyes are ever so
haughty, whose glances are so dis-
dainful;
14 those whose teeth are swords and
whose jaws are set with knives to de-

ever so 매우, 몹시
He sat there ever so quietly. 그는 거기에 너무도 조용히 앉아 있었다.

vour the poor from the earth and
the needy from among mankind.
15 "The leech has two daughters. 'Give!
Give!' they cry. "There are three
things that are never satisfied, four
that never say, 'Enough!':
16 the grave, the barren womb, land,
which is never satisfied with water,
and fire, which never says, 'Enough!'
17 "The eye that mocks a father, that
scorns an aged mother, will be
pecked out by the ravens of the val-
ley, will be eaten by the vultures.
18 "There are three things that are too
amazing for me, four that I do not
understand:

be satisfied with …에 만족하다
You should be satisfied with what you've got. 가진 것에 만족해야 합니다.

19 the way of an eagle in the sky, the
way of a snake on a rock, the way
of a ship on the high seas, and the
way of a man with a young woman.
20 "This is the way of an adulterous
woman: She eats and wipes her
mouth and says, 'I've done noth-
ing wrong.'
21 "Under three things the earth
trembles, under four it cannot bear
up:
22 a servant who becomes king, a godl-
ess fool who gets plenty to eat,
23 a contemptible woman who gets
married, and a servant who dis-
places her mistress.

bear up …을 견디다
I think I can bear up under it. 난 그것을 견딜 수 있다고 생각해.

24 "Four things on earth are small, yet
they are extremely wise:
25 Ants are creatures of little strength,
yet they store up their food in the
summer;
26 hyraxes are creatures of little power,
yet they make their home in the
crags;
27 locusts have no king, yet they
advance together in ranks;
28 a lizard can be caught with the hand,
yet it is found in kings' palaces.
29 "There are three things that are
stately in their stride, four that move
with stately bearing:
30 a lion, mighty among beasts, who

store up 비축하다
Store up to 6 months in a cool place. 그늘진 곳에 6달 동안 저장해라.

retreats before nothing;
31 a strutting rooster, a he-goat, and
a king secure against revolt.
32 "If you play the fool and exalt yours-
elf, or if you plan evil, clap your hand
over your mouth!
33 For as churning cream produces
butter, and as twisting the nose pro-
duces blood, so stirring up anger
produces strife."

Proverbs 31장 1~31절

1 The sayings of King Lemuel—an
inspired utterance his mother
taught him.

secure against …에 대비해서 지키다
We were secure against fire. 우리에게는 화재 위험이 없었다.

2 Listen, my son! Listen, son of my
womb! Listen, my son, the answer
to my prayers!
3 Do not spend your strength on
women, your vigor on those who
ruin kings.
4 It is not for kings, Lemuel—it is
not for kings to drink wine, not for
rulers to crave beer,
5 lest they drink and forget what has
been decreed, and deprive all the
oppressed of their rights.
6 Let beer be for those who are
perishing, wine for those who are in
anguish!
7 Let them drink and forget their

in anguish 슬퍼서
He groaned in anguish. 그가 몹시 괴로워하며 신음했다.

poverty and remember their mis-
ery no more.
8 Speak up for those who cannot
speak for themselves, for the rights
of all who are destitute.
9 Speak up and judge fairly; defend
the rights of the poor and needy.
10 A wife of noble character who can
find? She is worth far more than ru-
bies.
11 Her husband has full confidence in
her and lacks nothing of value.
12 She brings him good, not harm, all
the days of her life.
13 She selects wool and flax and works
with eager hands.

speak up for …을 강력하게 변호하다
I want to speak up for her. 나는 그녀를 위해 얘기하고 싶다.

14 She is like the merchant ships,
bringing her food from afar.
15 She gets up while it is still night; she
provides food for her family and por-
tions for her female servants.
16 She considers a field and buys it; out
of her earnings she plants a vine-
yard.
17 She sets about her work vigorously;
her arms are strong for her tasks.
18 She sees that her trading is profi-
table, and her lamp does not go out
at night.
19 In her hand she holds the distaff and
grasps the spindle with her fingers.
20 She opens her arms to the poor and

set about one's work 일에 착수하다
She sets about her work with joy and singing. 그녀는 기쁨과 노래로 일을 시작한다.

extends her hands to the needy.
21 When it snows, she has no fear for
her household; for all of them are
clothed in scarlet.
22 She makes coverings for her bed;
she is clothed in fine linen and
purple.
23 Her husband is respected at the city
gate, where he takes his seat among
the elders of the land.
24 She makes linen garments and sells
them, and supplies the merchants
with sashes.
25 She is clothed with strength and
dignity; she can laugh at the days
to come.

have no fear 무서움이 없다
He has no fear. 그는 무서움을 모른다.

26 She speaks with wisdom, and faithf-
ul instruction is on her tongue.
27 She watches over the affairs of her
household and does not eat the
bread of idleness.
28 Her children arise and call her
blessed; her husband also, and he
praises her:
29 "Many women do noble things, but
you surpass them all."
30 Charm is deceptive, and beauty is
fleeting; but a woman who fears the
LORD is to be praised.
31 Honor her for all that her hands have
done, and let her works bring her
praise at the city gate.

for all that …에도 불구하고
It is true for all that. 그래도 그것은 사실이다.

NIV개정

지혜의 성경 영어 잠언 따라쓰기 2

부록

잠언 16장~31장 / 원어민 발음 / 한글개역개정 수록

✦ 알파벳 대문자, 소문자, 발음기호와 발음

A a [eɪ] 에이	**B b** [bi:] 비	**C c** [si:] 시	**D d** [di:] 디
E e [i:] 이	**F f** [ef] 에프	**G g** [dʒi:] 지	**H h** [eɪtʃ] 에이치
I i [aɪ] 아이	**J j** [dʒeɪ] 제이	**K k** [keɪ] 케이	**L l** [el] 엘
M m [em] 엠	**N n** [en] 엔	**O o** [oʊ] 오	**P p** [pi:] 피
Q q [kju:] 큐	**R r** [ɑ:(r)] 아르	**S s** [es] 에스	**T t** [ti:] 티
U u [ju:] 유	**V v** [vi:] 브이	**W w** [ˈdʌblju:] 더블유	**X x** [eks] 엑스
Y y [waɪ] 와이	**Z z** [zed/zi:] 지		

Proverbs 잠언

16장 1 To humans belong the plans of the heart, but from the LORD comes the proper answer of the tongue.
투 휴먼즈 빌롱 더 플랜즈 어브 더 하아트, 벗 프럼 더 로어드 컴즈 더 프라퍼 앤서 어브 더 텅.
마음의 경영은 사람에게 있어도 말의 응답은 여호와께로부터 나오느니라

2 All a person's ways seem pure to them, but motives are weighed by the LORD.
올 어 퍼선즈 웨이즈 심 퓨 투 뎀, 벗 모우티브즈 아아 웨이드 바이 더 로어드.
사람의 행위가 자기 보기에는 모두 깨끗하여도 여호와는 심령을 감찰하시느니라

3 Commit to the LORD whatever you do, and he will establish your plans.
커밋 투 더 로어드 워테버 유 두, 언드 히 윌 이스태블리쉬 요어 플랜즈.
너의 행사를 여호와께 맡기라 그리하면 네가 경영하는 것이 이루어지리라

4 The LORD works out everything to its proper end—even the wicked for a day of disaster.
더 로어드 웍스 아웃 에브리씽 투 잇스 프라퍼 엔드 이빈 더 위커드 포어 어 데이 어브 디재스터.
여호와께서 온갖 것을 그 쓰임에 적당하게 지으셨나니 악인도 악한 날에 적당하게 하셨느니라

5 The LORD detests all the proud of heart. Be sure of this: They will not go unpunished.
더 로어드 디테스트스 올 더 프라우드 어브 하아트. 비 슈어 어브 디스 데이 윌 낫 고우 언퍼니쉬트.
무릇 마음이 교만한 자를 여호와께서 미워하시나니 피차 손을 잡을지라도 벌을 면하지 못하리라

6 Through love and faithfulness sin is atoned for; through the fear of the LORD evil is avoided.
쓰루 러브 언드 페이쓰펄네스 신 이즈 어토운드 포어 쓰루 더 피어 어브 더 로어드 이벌 이즈 어보이디드.
인자와 진리로 인하여 죄악이 속하게 되고 여호와를 경외함으로 말미암아 악에서 떠나게 되느니라

7 When the LORD takes pleasure in anyone's way, he causes their enemies to make peace with them.
웬 더 로어드 테익스 플레저 인 에니원즈 웨이, 히 카저즈 데어 에너미즈 투 메익 피스 윋 뎀.
사람의 행위가 여호와를 기쁘시게 하면 그 사람의 원수라도 그와 더불어 화목하게 하시느니라

8 Better a little with righteousness than much gain with injustice.
베터 어 리털 윋 라이처스너스 던 머치 게인 윋 인저스티스.
적은 소득이 공의를 겸하면 많은 소득이 불의를 겸한 것보다 나으니라

9 In their hearts humans plan their course, but the LORD establishes their steps.
인 데어 하아트스 휴먼즈 플랜 데어 코어스, 벗 더 로어드 이스태블리쉬즈 데어 스텝스.
사람이 마음으로 자기의 길을 계획할지라도 그의 걸음을 인도하시는 이는 여호와시니라

10 The lips of a king speak as an oracle, and his mouth does not betray justice.
더 립스 어브 어 킹 스픽 애즈 앤 오어러컬, 언드 히즈 마우쓰 더즈 낫 빗레이 저스터스.
하나님의 말씀이 왕의 입술에 있은즉 재판할 때에 그의 입이 그르치지 아니하리라

11 Honest scales and balances belong to the LORD; all the weights in the bag are of his making.
아너스트 스케일즈 언드 밸런시즈 빌롱 투 더 로어드 올 더 웨잇스 인 더 배그 아아 어브 히즈 메이킹.
공평한 저울과 접시 저울은 여호와의 것이요 주머니 속의 저울추도 다 그가 지으신 것이니라

12 Kings detest wrongdoing, for a throne is established through righteousness.
킹즈 디테스트 롱두잉, 포어 어 쓰로운 이즈 이스태블리쉬트 쓰루 라이처스너스.
악을 행하는 것은 왕들이 미워할 바니 이는 그 보좌가 공의로 말미암아 굳게 섬이니라

13 Kings take pleasure in honest lips; they value the one who speaks what is right.
킹즈 테익 플레저 인 아너스트 립스 데이 밸류 더 원 후 스픽스 웟 이즈 라이트.
의로운 입술은 왕들이 기뻐하는 것이요 정직하게 말하는 자는 그들의 사랑을 입느니라

14 A king's wrath is a messenger of death, but the wise will appease it.
어 킹즈 래쓰 이즈 어 메선저 어브 데쓰, 벗 더 와이즈 윌 어피즈 잇.
왕의 진노는 죽음의 사자들과 같아도 지혜로운 사람은 그것을 쉬게 하리라

15 When a king's face brightens, it means life; his favor is like a rain cloud in spring.
웬 어 킹즈 페이스 브라이튼즈, 잇 민즈 라이프 히즈 페이버 이즈 라익 어 레인 클라우드 인 스프링.
왕의 희색은 생명을 뜻하나니 그의 은택이 늦은 비를 내리는 구름과 같으니라

16 How much better to get wisdom than gold, to get insight rather than silver!
하우 머치 베터 투 겟 위즈덤 던 고울드, 투 겟 인사이트 래더 던 실버!
지혜를 얻는 것이 금을 얻는 것보다 얼마나 나은고 명철을 얻는 것이 은을 얻는 것보다 더욱 나으니라

17 The highway of the upright avoids evil; those who guard their ways preserve their lives.
더 하이웨이 어브 디 업라이트 어보이즈 이블 도우즈 후 가아드 데어 웨이즈 프러저브 데어 라이브즈.
악을 떠나는 것은 정직한 사람의 대로이니 자기의 길을 지키는 자는 자기의 영혼을 보전하느니라

18 Pride goes before destruction, a haughty spirit before a fall.
프라이드 고우즈 비포어 디스트럭션, 어 호티스 피럿 비포어 어 폴.
교만은 패망의 선봉이요 거만한 마음은 넘어짐의 앞잡이니라

19 Better to be lowly in spirit along with the oppressed than to share plunder with the proud.
베터 투 비 로울리 인 스피릿 얼롱 윋 디 업레스트 던 투 셰어 플런더 윋 더 프라우드.
겸손한 자와 함께 하여 마음을 낮추는 것이 교만한 자와 함께 하여 탈취물을 나누는 것보다 나으니라

20 Whoever gives heed to instruction prospers, and blessed is the one who trusts in the LORD.
후에버 기브즈 히드 투 인스트럭션 프라스퍼즈, 언드 블레스트 이즈 더 원 후 트러스트스 인 더 로어드.
삼가 말씀에 주의하는 자는 좋은 것을 얻나니 여호와를 의지하는 자는 복이 있느니라

21 The wise in heart are called discerning, and gracious words promote instruction.
더 와이즈 인 하아트 아아 콜드 디서닝, 언드 그레이셔스 워즈 프러모우트 인스트럭션.
마음이 지혜로운 자는 명철하다 일컬음을 받고 입이 선한 자는 남의 학식을 더하게 하느니라

22 Prudence is a fountain of life to the prudent, but folly brings punishment to fools.
프루던스 이즈 어 파운턴 어브 라이프 투 더 프루던트, 벗 팔리 브링즈 퍼니쉬먼트 투 풀즈.
명철한 자에게는 그 명철이 생명의 샘이 되거니와 미련한 자에게는 그 미련한 것이 징계가 되느니라

23 The hearts of the wise make their mouths prudent, and their lips promote instruction.
더 하아트스 어브 더 와이즈 메익 데어 마운즈 프루던트, 언드 데어 립스 프러모우트 인스트럭션.
지혜로운 자의 마음은 그의 입을 슬기롭게 하고 또 그의 입술에 지식을 더하느니라

24 Gracious words are a honeycomb, sweet to the soul and healing to the bones.
그레이셔스 워즈 아아 어 허니코움, 스윗 투 더 소울 언드 힐링 투 더 보운즈.
선한 말은 꿀송이 같아서 마음에 달고 뼈에 양약이 되느니라

25 There is a way that appears to be right, but in the end it leads to death.
데어 이즈 어 웨이 댓 어피어즈 투 비 라이트, 벗 인 디 엔드 잇 리즈 투 데쓰.

어떤 길은 사람이 보기에 바르나 필경은 사망의 길이니라

26 The appetite of laborers works for them; their hunger drives them on.
디 애퍼타이트 어브 레이버러즈 웍스 포어 뎀 데어 헝거 드라이브즈 뎀 안.
고되게 일하는 자는 식욕으로 말미암아 애쓰나니 이는 그의 입이 자기를 독촉함이니라

27 A scoundrel plots evil, and on their lips it is like a scorching fire.
어 스카운드럴 플랏스 이벌, 언드 안 데어 립스 잇 이즈 라익 어 스코어칭 파여.
불량한 자는 악을 꾀하나니 그 입술에는 맹렬한 불 같은 것이 있느니라

28 A perverse person stirs up conflict, and a gossip separates close friends.
어 퍼버스 퍼선 스터즈 업 칸플릭트, 언드 어 가섭 세퍼릿스 클로우스 프렌즈.
패역한 자는 다툼을 일으키고 말쟁이는 친한 벗을 이간하느니라

29 A violent person entices their neighbor and leads them down a path that is not good.
어 바이얼런트 퍼선 인타이서즈 데어 네이버 언드 리즈 뎀 다운 어 패쓰 댓 이즈 낫 구드.
강포한 사람은 그 이웃을 꾀어 좋지 아니한 길로 인도하느니라

30 Whoever winks with their eye is plotting perversity; whoever purses their lips is bent on evil.
후에버 윙크스 윋 데어 아이 이즈 플라팅 퍼버서티 후에버 퍼시즈 데어 립스 이즈 벤트 안 이벌.
눈짓을 하는 자는 패역한 일을 도모하며 입술을 닫는 자는 악한 일을 이루느니라

31 Gray hair is a crown of splendor; it is attained in the way of righteousness.
그레이 헤어 이즈 어 크라운 어브 스플렌더 잇 이즈 어테인드 인 더 웨이 어브 라이처스너스.
백발은 영화의 면류관이라 공의로운 길에서 얻으리라

32 Better a patient person than a warrior, one with self-control than one who takes a city.
베터 어 페이션트 퍼선 던 어 워리어, 원 윋 셀프컨트로울 던 원 후 테익스 어 시티.
노하기를 더디하는 자는 용사보다 낫고 자기의 마음을 다스리는 자는 성을 빼앗는 자보다 나으니라

33 The lot is cast into the lap, but its every decision is from the LORD.
더 랏 이즈 캐스트 인투 더 랩, 벗 잇스 에브리 디시전 이즈 프럼 더 로어드.
제비는 사람이 뽑으나 모든 일을 작정하기는 여호와께 있느니라

human [hjúːmən] a. 사람의
belong [bilɔ́(ː)ŋ] vi. 속하다
proper [prɑ́pər] a. 적당한
pure [pjuər] a. 순수한
motive [móutiv] n. 동기, 원인
atone [ətóun] vi. 속하다
cause [kɔːz] n. 원인, 이유
pleasure [pléʒər] n. 기쁨
righteous [ráitʃəs] a. 올바른
injustice [indʒʌ́stis] n. 부정
oracle [ɔ́(ː)rəkəl] n. 신탁
betray [bitréi] vt. 배반하다
punishment [pʌ́niʃmənt] n. 벌
balance [bǽləns] n. 저울
fool [fuːl] n. 바보
throne [θroun] n. 왕좌, 옥좌
messenger [mésəndʒər] n. 사자
brighten [bráitn] vt. 빛내다
appease [əpíːz] vt. 달래다
scoundrel [skáundrəl] n. 악당
cloud [klaud] n. 구름
spring [spriŋ] n. 봄
warrior [wɔ́(ː)riər] n. 전사
decision [disíʒən] n. 결정, 판단

17장 1 Better a dry crust with peace and quiet than a house full of feasting, with strife.
베터 어 드라이 크러스트 윋 피스 언드 콰엇 던 어 하우스 풀 어브 피스팅, 윋 스트라이프.
마른 떡 한 조각만 있고도 화목하는 것이 제육이 집에 가득하고도 다투는 것보다 나으니라

2 A prudent servant will rule over a disgraceful son and will share the inheritance as one of the family.
어 프루던트 서번트 윌 룰 오우버 어 디스그레이스펄 선 언드 윌 셰어 디 인헤러턴스 애즈 원 어브 더 패멀리.

슬기로운 종은 부끄러운 짓을 하는 주인의 아들을 다스리겠고 또 형제들 중에서 유업을 나누어 얻으리라

3 The crucible for silver and the furnace for gold, but the LORD tests the heart.

더 크루서벌 포어 실버 언드 더 퍼너스 포어 고울드, 벗 더 로어드 테스트스 더 하아트.

도가니는 은을, 풀무는 금을 연단하거니와 여호와는 마음을 연단하시느니라

4 A wicked person listens to deceitful lips; a liar pays attention to a destructive tongue.

어 위커드 퍼선 리선즈 투 디싯펄 립스 어 라여 페이즈 어텐션 투 어 디스트럭티브 텅.

악을 행하는 자는 사악한 입술이 하는 말을 잘 듣고 거짓말을 하는 자는 악한 혀가 하는 말에 귀를 기울이느니라

5 Whoever mocks the poor shows contempt for their Maker; whoever gloats over disaster will not go unpunished.

후에버 막스 더 푸어 쇼우즈 컨템프트 포어 데어 메이커 후에버 글로웃스 오우버 디재스터 윌 낫 고우 언퍼니쉬트.

가난한 자를 조롱하는 자는 그를 지으신 주를 멸시하는 자요 사람의 재앙을 기뻐하는 자는 형벌을 면하지 못할 자니라

6 Children's children are a crown to the aged, and parents are the pride of their children.

칠드런즈 칠드런 아아 어 크라운 투 디 에이지드, 언드 페런트스 아아 더 프라이드 어브 데어 칠드런.

손자는 노인의 면류관이요 아비는 자식의 영화니라

7 Eloquent lips are unsuited to a godless fool—how much worse lying lips to a ruler!

엘러퀀트 립스 아아 언수티드 투 어 가들러스 풀 하우 머치 워스 라이잉 립스 투 어 룰러!

지나친 말을 하는 것도 미련한 자에게 합당하지 아니하거든 하물며 거짓말을 하는 것이 존귀한 자에게 합당하겠느냐

8 A bribe is seen as a charm by the one who gives it; they think success will come at every turn.

어 브라이브 이즈 신 애즈 어 참 바이 더 원 후 기브즈 잇 데이 씽크 석세스 윌 컴 앳 에브리 턴.

뇌물은 그 임자가 보기에 보석 같은즉 그가 어디로 향하든지 형통하게 하느니라

9 Whoever would foster love covers over an offense, but whoever repeats the matter separates close friends.

후에버 워드 파스터 러브 커버즈 오우버 앤 어펜스, 벗 후에버 리핏스 더 매터 세퍼릿스 클로우스 프렌즈.

허물을 덮어 주는 자는 사랑을 구하는 자요 그것을 거듭 말하는 자는 친한 벗을 이간하는 자니라

10.A rebuke impresses a discerning person more than a hundred lashes a fool.

어 리뷰 임프레시즈 어 디서닝 퍼선 모어 던 어 헌드러드 래쉬즈 어 풀.

한 마디 말로 총명한 자에게 충고하는 것이 매 백 대로 미련한 자를 때리는 것보다 더욱 깊이 박히느니라

11 Evildoers foster rebellion against God; the messenger of death will be sent against them.

이벌두어즈 파스터 리벨련 어겐스트 가드 더 메선저 어브 데쓰 윌 비 센트 어겐스트 뎀.

악한 자는 반역만 힘쓰나니 그러므로 그에게 잔인한 사자가 보냄을 받으리라

12 Better to meet a bear robbed of her cubs than a fool bent on folly.

베터 투 밋 어 베어 라브드 어브 허 커브즈 던 어 풀 벤트 안 팔리.

차라리 새끼 빼앗긴 암곰을 만날지언정 미련한 일을 행하는 미련한 자를 만나지 말 것이니라

13 Evil will never leave the house of one who pays back evil for good.

이벌 윌 네버 리브 더 하우스 어브 원 후 페이즈 백 이벌 포어 구드.

누구든지 악으로 선을 갚으면 악이 그 집을 떠나지 아니하리라

14 Starting a quarrel is like breaching a dam; so drop the matter before a dispute breaks out.

스타아팅 어 쿼럴 이즈 라익 브리칭 어 댐 소우 드랍 더 매터 비포어 어 디스퓨 브레익스 아웃.
다투는 시작은 둑에서 물이 새는 것 같은즉 싸움이 일어나기 전에 시비를 그칠 것이니라

15 Acquitting the guilty and condemning the innocent—the LORD detests them both.
어퀴팅 더 길티 언드 컨데밍 디 이너선트 더 로어드 디테스트스 뎀 보우쓰.
악인을 의롭다 하고 의인을 악하다 하는 이 두 사람은 다 여호와께 미움을 받느니라

16 Why should fools have money in hand to buy wisdom, when they are not able to understand it?
와이 슈드 풀즈 해브 머니 인 핸드 투 바이 위즈덤, 웬 데이 아아 낫 에이벌 투 언더스탠드 잇?
미련한 자는 무지하거늘 손에 값을 가지고 지혜를 사려 함은 어찜인고

17 A friend loves at all times, and a brother is born for a time of adversity.
어 프렌드 러브즈 앳 올 타임즈, 언드 어 브러더 이즈 본 포어 어 타임 어브 애드버시티.
친구는 사랑이 끊어지지 아니하고 형제는 위급한 때를 위하여 났느니라

18 One who has no sense shakes hands in pledge and puts up security for a neighbor.
원 후 해즈 노우 센스 셰익스 핸즈 인 플레지 언드 풋스 업 시큐러티 포어 어 네이버.
지혜 없는 자는 남의 손을 잡고 그의 이웃 앞에서 보증이 되느니라

19 Whoever loves a quarrel loves sin; whoever builds a high gate invites destruction.
후에버 러브즈 어 쿼럴 러브즈 신 후에버 빌즈 어 하이 게이트 인바잇스 디스트럭션.
다툼을 좋아하는 자는 죄과를 좋아하는 자요 자기 문을 높이는 자는 파괴를 구하는 자니라

20 One whose heart is corrupt does not prosper; one whose tongue is perverse falls into trouble.
원 후즈 하아트 이즈 커럽트 더즈 낫 프라스퍼 원 후즈 텅 이즈 퍼버스 폴즈 인투 트러벌.
마음이 굽은 자는 복을 얻지 못하고 혀가 패역한 자는 재앙에 빠지느니라

21 To have a fool for a child brings grief; there is no joy for the parent of a godless fool.
투 해브 어 풀 포어 어 차일드 브링즈 그리프 데어 이즈 노우 조이 포어 더 페런트 어브 어 가들러스 풀.
미련한 자를 낳는 자는 근심을 당하나니 미련한 자의 아비는 낙이 없느니라

22 A cheerful heart is good medicine, but a crushed spirit dries up the bones.
어 치어펄 하아트 이즈 구드 메더선, 벗 어 크러쉬트 스피럿 드라이즈 업 더 보운즈.
마음의 즐거움은 양약이라도 심령의 근심은 뼈를 마르게 하느니라

23 The wicked accept bribes in secret to pervert the course of justice.
더 위커드 억셉트 브라이브즈 인 시크럿 투 퍼버트 더 코어스 어브 저스터스.
악인은 사람의 품에서 뇌물을 받고 재판을 굽게 하느니라

24 A discerning person keeps wisdom in view, but a fool's eyes wander to the ends of the earth.
어 디서닝 퍼선 킵스 위즈덤 인 뷰, 벗 어 풀즈 아이즈 완더 투 디 엔즈 어브 디 어쓰.
지혜는 명철한 자 앞에 있거늘 미련한 자는 눈을 땅 끝에 두느니라

25 A foolish son brings grief to his father and bitterness to the mother who bore him.
어 풀리쉬 선 브링즈 그리프 투 히즈 파더 언드 비터너스 투 더 머더 후 보어 힘.
미련한 아들은 그 아비의 근심이 되고 그 어미의 고통이 되느니라

26 If imposing a fine on the innocent is not good, surely to flog honest officials is not right.
이프 임포우징 어 파인 안 디 이너선트 이즈 낫 구드, 슈얼리 투 플라그 아너스트 어피셜즈 이즈 낫 라이트.
의인을 벌하는 것과 귀인을 정직하다고 때리는 것은 선하지 못하니라

27 The one who has knowledge uses words with restraint, and whoever has understanding is even-tempered.
더 원 후 해즈 날러지 유저즈 워즈 윋 리스트레인트, 언드 후에버 해즈 언더스탠딩 이즈 이빈템퍼드.
말을 아끼는 자는 지식이 있고 성품이 냉철한 자는 명철하니라

28 Even fools are thought wise if they keep silent, and discerning if they hold their tongues.
이빈 풀즈 아아 쏫 와이즈 이프 데이 킵 사일런트, 언드 디서닝 이프 데이 호울드 데어 텅즈.
미련한 자라도 잠잠하면 지혜로운 자로 여겨지고 그의 입술을 닫으면 슬기로운 자로 여겨지느니라

crust [krʌst] n. 빵 껍질	pay [pei] vt. 갚다, 상환하다	rebellion [ribéljən] n. 모반
quiet [kwáiət] a. 조용한	show [ʃou] vt. 보이다, 제시하다	against [əgénst] prep. …을 향하여
feast [fiːst] n. 축제	gloat [glout] vi. 흡족한	dispute [dispjúːt] vi. 논쟁하다
rule [ruːl] n. 규칙, 규정	eloquent [éləkwənt] a. 웅변의	guilty [gílti] a. 유죄의
crucible [krúːsəbl] n. 도가니	offense [əféns] n. 위반, 불법	keep [kiːp] vt. 계속하다
furnace [fə́ːrnis] n. 아궁이	repeat [ripíːt] vt. 되풀이하다	adversity [ædvə́ːrsəti] n. 역경
listen [lísən] vi. 귀를 기울이다	discern [disə́ːrn] vt. 분별하다	acquit [əkwít] vt. 석방하다
liar [láiər] n. 거짓말쟁이	lash [læʃ] n. 채찍의 휘는 부분	silent [sáilənt] a. 침묵하는

18장 1 An unfriendly person pursues selfish ends and against all sound judgment starts quarrels.
앤 언프렌들리 퍼선 퍼수즈 셀피쉬 엔즈 언드 어겐스트 올 사운드 저지먼트 스타아트 스쿼럴즈.
무리에게서 스스로 갈라지는 자는 자기 소욕을 따르는 자라 온갖 참 지혜를 배척하느니라

2 Fools find no pleasure in understanding but delight in airing their own opinions.
풀즈 파인드 노우 플레저 인 언더스탠딩 벗 딜랏 인 에어링 데어 오운 어피년즈.
미련한 자는 명철을 기뻐하지 아니하고 자기의 의사를 드러내기만 기뻐하느니라

3 When wickedness comes, so does contempt, and with shame comes reproach.
웬 위커드너스 컴즈, 소우 더즈 컨템프트, 언드 윋 셰임 컴즈 립로우치.
악한 자가 이를 때에는 멸시도 따라오고 부끄러운 것이 이를 때에는 능욕도 함께 오느니라

4 The words of the mouth are deep waters, but the fountain of wisdom is a rushing stream.
더 워즈 어브 더 마우쓰 아아 딥 워터즈, 벗 더 파운턴 어브 위즈덤 이즈 어 러쉉 스트림.
명철한 사람의 입의 말은 깊은 물과 같고 지혜의 샘은 솟구쳐 흐르는 내와 같으니라

5 It is not good to be partial to the wicked and so deprive the innocent of justice.
잇 이즈 낫 구드 투 비 파아셜 투 더 위커드 언드 소우 딥라이브 디 이너선트 어브 저스터스.
악인을 두둔하는 것과 재판할 때에 의인을 억울하게 하는 것이 선하지 아니하니라

6 The lips of fools bring them strife, and their mouths invite a beating.
더 립스 어브 풀즈 브링 뎀 스트라이프, 언드 데어 마욷즈 인바이트 어 비팅.
미련한 자의 입술은 다툼을 일으키고 그의 입은 매를 자청하느니라

7 The mouths of fools are their undoing, and their lips are a snare to their very lives.
더 마욷즈 어브 풀즈 아아 데어 언두잉, 언드 데어 립스 아아 어 스네어 투 데어 베어리 라이브즈.
미련한 자의 입은 그의 멸망이 되고 그의 입술은 그의 영혼의 그물이 되느니라

8 The words of a gossip are like choice morsels; they go down to the inmost parts.
더 워즈 어브 어 가섭 아아 라익 초이스 모어설즈 데이 고우 다운 투 디 인모우스트 파아트스.

남의 말하기를 좋아하는 자의 말은 별식과 같아서 뱃속 깊은 데로 내려가느니라

9 One who is slack in his work is brother to one who destroys.
원 후 이즈 슬랙 인 히즈 웍 이즈 브러더 투 원 후 디스트로이즈.
자기의 일을 게을리하는 자는 패가하는 자의 형제니라

10 The name of the LORD is a fortified tower; the righteous run to it and are safe.
더 네임 어브 더 로어드 이즈 어 포어터파이드 타워 더 라이처스 런 투 잇 언드 아아 세이프.
여호와의 이름은 견고한 망대라 의인은 그리로 달려가서 안전함을 얻느니라

11 The wealth of the rich is their fortified city; they imagine it a wall too high to scale.
더 웰쓰 어브 더 리치 이즈 데어 포어터파이드 시티 데이 이매전 잇 어 월 투 하이 투 스케일.
부자의 재물은 그의 견고한 성이라 그가 높은 성벽 같이 여기느니라

12 Before a downfall the heart is haughty, but humility comes before honor.
비포어 어 다운폴 더 하아트 이즈 호티, 벗 휴밀리티 컴즈 비포어 아너.
사람의 마음의 교만은 멸망의 선봉이요 겸손은 존귀의 길잡이니라

13 To answer before listening—that is folly and shame.
투 앤서 비포어 리서닝 댓 이즈 팔리 언드 세임.
사연을 듣기 전에 대답하는 자는 미련하여 욕을 당하느니라

14 The human spirit can endure in sickness, but a crushed spirit who can bear?
더 휴먼 스피럿 캔 엔듀 인 식너스, 벗 어 크러쉬트 스피럿 후 캔 베어?
사람의 심령은 그의 병을 능히 이기려니와 심령이 상하면 그것을 누가 일으키겠느냐

15 The heart of the discerning acquires knowledge, for the ears of the wise seek it out.
더 하아트 어브 더 디서닝 어콰이어즈 날러지, 포어 디 이어즈 어브 더 와이즈 식 잇 아웃.
명철한 자의 마음은 지식을 얻고 지혜로운 자의 귀는 지식을 구하느니라

16 A gift opens the way and ushers the giver into the presence of the great.
어 기프트 오우펀즈 더 웨이 언드 어셔즈 더 기버 인투 더 프레전스 어브 더 그레이트.
사람의 선물은 그의 길을 넓게 하며 또 존귀한 자 앞으로 그를 인도하느니라

17 In a lawsuit the first to speak seems right, until someone comes forward and cross-examines.
인 어 로숫 더 퍼스트 투 스픽 심즈 라이트, 언틸 서원 컴즈 포어루어드 언드 크로스이그재먼즈.
송사에서는 먼저 온 사람의 말이 바른 것 같으나 그의 상대자가 와서 밝히느니라

18 Casting the lot settles disputes and keeps strong opponents apart.
캐스팅 더 랏 세털즈 디스퓻스 언드 킵스 스트롱 어포우넌트스 어파아트.
제비 뽑는 것은 다툼을 그치게 하여 강한 자 사이에 해결하게 하느니라

19 A brother wronged is more unyielding than a fortified city; disputes are like the barred gates of a citadel.
어 브러더 롱드 이즈 모어 어닐딩 던 어 포어터파이드 시티 디스퓻스 아아 라익 더 바아드 게잇스 어브 어 시터델.
노엽게 한 형제와 화목하기가 견고한 성을 취하기보다 어려운즉 이러한 다툼은 산성 문빗장 같으니라

20 From the fruit of their mouth a person's stomach is filled; with the harvest of their lips they are satisfied.
프럼 더 프룻 어브 데어 마우쓰 어 퍼선즈 스터먹 이즈 필드 윋 더 하아버스트 어브 데어 립스 데이 아아 새터스파

이드.
사람은 입에서 나오는 열매로 말미암아 배부르게 되나니 곧 그의 입술에서 나는 것으로 말미암아 만족하게 되느니라

21 The tongue has the power of life and death, and those who love it will eat its fruit.
더 텅 해즈 더 파워 어브 라이프 언드 데쓰, 언드 도우즈 후 러브 잇 윌 잇 잇스 프룻.
죽고 사는 것이 혀의 힘에 달렸나니 혀를 쓰기 좋아하는 자는 혀의 열매를 먹으리라

22 He who finds a wife finds what is good and receives favor from the LORD.
히 후 파인즈 어 와이프 파인즈 웟 이즈 구드 언드 러시브즈 페이버 프럼 더 로어드.
아내를 얻는 자는 복을 얻고 여호와께 은총을 받는 자니라

23 The poor plead for mercy, but the rich answer harshly.
더 푸어 플리드 포어 머시, 벗 더 리치 앤서 하아슬리.
가난한 자는 간절한 말로 구하여도 부자는 엄한 말로 대답하느니라

24 One who has unreliable friends soon comes to ruin, but there is a friend who sticks closer than a brother.
원 후 해즈 언릴라이어벌 프렌즈 순 컴즈 투 루언, 벗 데어 이즈 어 프렌드 후 스틱스 클로우서 던 어 브러더.
많은 친구를 얻는 자는 해를 당하게 되거니와 어떤 친구는 형제보다 친밀하니라

selfish [sélfiʃ] a. 이기적인	partial [pɑ́ːrʃəl] a. 부분적인	opponent [əpóunənt] a. 반대하는
end [end] n. 끝, 결말	justice [dʒʌ́stis] n. 정의, 공정	citadel [sítədl] n. 성채, 요새
sound [saund] n. 소리, 음	beat [biːt] vt. 치다	city [síti] n. 도시, 도회
start [stɑːrt] vi. 출발하다	morsel [mɔ́ːrsəl] n. 가벼운 식사	wall [wɔːl] n. 벽, 담
stomach [stʌ́mək] n. 위	slack [slæk] a. 느슨한	high [hái] a. 높은
opinion [əpínjən] n. 의견, 견해	brother [brʌ́ðər] n. 남자 형제, 형	downfall [ˈdaunfɔːl] n. 쏟아짐, 낙하
reproach [ripróutʃ] vt. 비난하다	tower [táuər] n. 탑, 망루	haughty [hɔ́ːti] a. 오만한, 거만한
stream [striːm] n. 시내, 개울	safe [seif] a. 안전한	acquire [əkwáiər] vt. 손에 넣다

19장 1 Better the poor whose walk is blameless than a fool whose lips are perverse.
베터 더 푸어 후즈 웍 이즈 블레임러스 던 어 풀 후즈 립스 아아 퍼버스.
가난하여도 성실하게 행하는 자는 입술이 패역하고 미련한 자보다 나으니라

2 Desire without knowledge is not good—how much more will hasty feet miss the way!
디자여 위다우트 날러지 이즈 낫 구드 하우 머치 모어 윌 헤이스티 핏 미스 더 웨이!
지식 없는 소원은 선하지 못하고 발이 급한 사람은 잘못 가느니라

3 A person's own folly leads to their ruin, yet their heart rages against the LORD.
어 퍼선즈 오운 팔리 리즈 투 데어 루언, 옛 데어 하아트 레이지즈 어겐스트 더 로어드.
사람이 미련하므로 자기 길을 굽게 하고 마음으로 여호와를 원망하느니라

4 Wealth attracts many friends, but even the closest friend of the poor person deserts them.
웰쓰 엇랙트스 메니 프렌즈, 벗 이빈 더 클로우서스트 프렌드 어브 더 푸어 퍼선 디저트스 뎀.
재물은 많은 친구를 더하게 하나 가난한즉 친구가 끊어지느니라

5 A false witness will not go unpunished, and whoever pours out lies will not go free.
어 폴스 윗너스 윌 낫 고우 언퍼니쉬트, 언드 후에버 포어즈 아웃 라이즈 윌 낫 고우 프리.
거짓 증인은 벌을 면하지 못할 것이요 거짓말을 하는 자도 피하지 못하리라

6 Many curry favor with a ruler, and everyone is the friend of one who gives gifts.
메니 커어리 페이버 윋 어 룰러, 언드 에브리원 이즈 더 프렌드 어브 원 후 기브즈 기프트스.
너그러운 사람에게는 은혜를 구하는 자가 많고 선물 주기를 좋아하는 자에게는 사람마다 친구가 되느니라

7 The poor are shunned by all their relatives—how much more do their friends avoid them! Though
the poor pursue them with pleading, they are nowhere to be found.
더 푸어 아아 션드 바이 올 데어 렐러티브즈 하우 머치 모어 두 데어 프렌즈 어보이드 뎀! 도우 더 푸어 펴수 뎀 윋 플리딩, 데이 아아 노우웨어 투 비 파운드.
가난한 자는 그의 형제들에게도 미움을 받거든 하물며 친구야 그를 멀리 하지 아니하겠느냐 따라가며 말하려 할지라도 그들이 없어졌으리라

8 The one who gets wisdom loves life; the one who cherishes understanding will soon prosper.
더 원 후 겟스 위즈덤 러브즈 라이프 더 원 후 체어리쉬즈 언더스탠딩 윌 순 프라스퍼.
지혜를 얻는 자는 자기 영혼을 사랑하고 명철을 지키는 자는 복을 얻느니라

9 A false witness will not go unpunished, and whoever pours out lies will perish.
어 폴스 윗너스 윌 낫 고우 언퍼니쉬트, 언드 후에버 포어즈 아웃 라이즈 윌 페어리쉬.
거짓 증인은 벌을 면하지 못할 것이요 거짓말을 뱉는 자는 망할 것이니라

10 It is not fitting for a fool to live in luxury—how much worse for a slave to rule over princes!
잇 이즈 낫 피팅 포어 어 풀 투 리브 인 러그저리 하우 머치 워스 포어 어 슬레이브 투 룰 오우버 프린서즈!
미련한 자가 사치하는 것이 적당하지 못하거든 하물며 종이 방백을 다스림이랴

11 A person's wisdom yields patience; it is to one's glory to overlook an offense.
어 퍼선즈 위즈덤 일즈 페이션스 잇 이즈 투 원즈 글로어리 투 오우벌룩 앤 어펜스.
노하기를 더디 하는 것이 사람의 슬기요 허물을 용서하는 것이 자기의 영광이니라

12 A king's rage is like the roar of a lion, but his favor is like dew on the grass.
어 킹즈 레이지 이즈 라익 더 로어 어브 어 라이언, 벗 히즈 페이버 이즈 라익 두 안 더 그래스.
왕의 노함은 사자의 부르짖음 같고 그의 은택은 풀 위의 이슬 같으니라

13 A foolish child is a father's ruin, and a quarrelsome wife is like the constant dripping of a leaky roof.
어 풀리쉬 차일드 이즈 어 파더즈 루언, 언드 어 쿼럴섬 와이프 이즈 라익 더 칸스턴트 드리핑 어브 어 리키 루프.
미련한 아들은 그의 아비의 재앙이요 다투는 아내는 이어 떨어지는 물방울이니라

14 Houses and wealth are inherited from parents, but a prudent wife is from the LORD.
하우서즈 언드 웰쓰 아아 인헤러티드 프럼 페런트스, 벗 어 프루던트 와이프 이즈 프럼 더 로어드.
집과 재물은 조상에게서 상속하거니와 슬기로운 아내는 여호와께로서 말미암느니라

15 Laziness brings on deep sleep, and the shiftless go hungry.
레이지너스 브링즈 안 딥 슬립, 언드 더 쉬프틀리스 고우 헝그리.
게으름이 사람으로 깊이 잠들게 하나니 태만한 사람은 주릴 것이니라

16 Whoever keeps commandments keeps their life, but whoever shows contempt for their ways will die.
후에버 킵스 커맨드먼트스 킵스 데어 라이프, 벗 후에버 쇼우즈 컨템프트 포어 데어 웨이즈 윌 다이.
계명을 지키는 자는 자기의 영혼을 지키거니와 자기의 행실을 삼가지 아니하는 자는 죽으리라

17 Whoever is kind to the poor lends to the LORD, and he will reward them for what they have done.
후에버 이즈 카인드 투 더 푸어 렌즈 투 더 로어드, 언드 히 윌 리워어드 뎀 포어 웟 데이 해브 던.

가난한 자를 불쌍히 여기는 것은 여호와께 꾸어 드리는 것이니 그의 선행을 그에게 갚아 주시리라

18 Discipline your children, for in that there is hope; do not be a willing party to their death.
디서플런 요어 칠드런, 포어 인 댓 데어 이즈 호웁 두 낫 비 어 윌링 파아티 투 데어 데쓰.
네가 네 아들에게 희망이 있은즉 그를 징계하되 죽일 마음은 두지 말지니라

19 A hot-tempered person must pay the penalty; rescue them, and you will have to do it again.
어 핫템퍼드 퍼선 머스트 페이 더 페널티 레스큐 뎀, 언드 유 윌 해브 투 두 잇 어겐.
노하기를 맹렬히 하는 자는 벌을 받을 것이라 네가 그를 건져 주면 다시 그런 일이 생기리라

20 Listen to advice and accept discipline, and at the end you will be counted among the wise.
리선 투 애드바이스 언드 억셉트 디서플런, 언드 앳 디 엔드 유 윌 비 카운티드 어멍 더 와이즈.
너는 권고를 들으며 훈계를 받으라 그리하면 네가 필경은 지혜롭게 되리라

21 Many are the plans in a person's heart, but it is the LORD's purpose that prevails.
메니 아아 더 플랜즈 인 어 퍼선즈 하아트, 벗 잇 이즈 더 로어즈 퍼퍼스 댓 프리베일즈.
사람의 마음에는 많은 계획이 있어도 오직 여호와의 뜻만이 완전히 서리라

22 What a person desires is unfailing love; better to be poor than a liar.
웟 어 퍼선 디자여즈 이즈 언페일링 러브 베터 투 비 푸어 던 어 라여.
사람은 자기의 인자함으로 남에게 사모함을 받느니라 가난한 자는 거짓말하는 자보다 나으니라

23 The fear of the LORD leads to life; then one rests content, untouched by trouble.
더 피어 어브 더 로어드 리즈 투 라이프 덴 원 레스트 스칸텐트, 언터치트 바이 트러벌.
여호와를 경외하는 것은 사람으로 생명에 이르게 하는 것이라 경외하는 자는 족하게 지내고 재앙을 당하지 아니하느니라

24 A sluggard buries his hand in the dish; he will not even bring it back to his mouth!
어 슬러거드 베어리즈 히즈 핸드 인 더 디쉬 히 윌 낫 이빈 브링 잇 백 투 히즈 마우쓰!
게으른 자는 자기의 손을 그릇에 넣고서도 입으로 올리기를 괴로워하느니라

25 Flog a mocker, and the simple will learn prudence; rebuke the discerning, and they will gain knowledge.
플라그 어 마커, 언드 더 심펄 윌 런 프루던스 리뷰크 더 디서닝, 언드 데이 윌 게인 날러지.
거만한 자를 때리라 그리하면 어리석은 자도 지혜를 얻으리라 명철한 자를 견책하라 그리하면 그가 지식을 얻으리라

26 Whoever robs their father and drives out their mother is a child who brings shame and disgrace.
후에버 라브즈 데어 파더 언드 드라이브즈 아웃 데어 머더 이즈 어 차일드 후 브링즈 셰임 언드 디스그레이스.
아비를 구박하고 어미를 쫓아내는 자는 부끄러움을 끼치며 능욕을 부르는 자식이니라

27 Stop listening to instruction, my son, and you will stray from the words of knowledge.
스탑 리서닝 투 인스트럭션, 마이 선, 언드 유 윌 스트레이 프럼 더 워즈 어브 날러지.
내 아들아 지식의 말씀에서 떠나게 하는 교훈을 듣지 말지니라

28 A corrupt witness mocks at justice, and the mouth of the wicked gulps down evil.
어 커럽트 윗너스 막스 앳 저스터스, 언드 더 마우쓰 어브 더 위커드 걸프스 다운 이벌.
망령된 증인은 정의를 업신여기고 악인의 입은 죄악을 삼키느니라

29 Penalties are prepared for mockers, and beatings for the backs of fools.

페널티즈 아아 프리페어드 포어 마커즈, 언드 비팅즈 포어 더 백스 어브 풀즈.
심판은 거만한 자를 위하여 예비된 것이요 채찍은 어리석은 자의 등을 위하여 예비된 것이니라

hasty [héisti] a. 급한
miss [mis] vt. 못 맞히다
own [oun] a. 자기 자신의
rage [reidʒ] n. 격노, 분격
attract [ətrǽkt] vt. 끌다
friend [frend] n. 벗, 친구
desert [dizə́ːrt] vt. 버리다
curry [kə́ːri] n. 카레가루
gift [gift] n. 선물, 선사품
more [mɔːr] a. 더 많은
plead [pliːd] vt. 변호하다
patience [péiʃəns] n. 인내
offense [əféns] n. 위반, 반칙
dew [djuː] n. 이슬, 방울
fitting [fítiŋ] a. 적당한, 꼭 맞는
luxury [lʌ́kʃəri] n. 사치, 호사
constant [kάnstənt] a. 변치 않는
leaky [líːki] a. 새기 쉬운
roof [ruːf] n. 지붕, 지붕 모양의 것
inherit [inhérit] vt. 상속하다
hungry [hʌ́ŋgri] a. 배고픈, 주린
prevail [privéil] vi. 우세하다
flog [flαg] vt. 매질하다
shame [ʃeim] n. 부끄럼

20장 1 Wine is a mocker and beer a brawler; whoever is led astray by them is not wise.
와인 이즈 어 마커 언드 비어 어 브롤러 후에버 이즈 레드 어스트레이 바이 뎀 이즈 낫 와이즈.
포도주는 거만하게 하는 것이요 독주는 떠들게 하는 것이라 이에 미혹되는 자마다 지혜가 없느니라

2 A king's wrath strikes terror like the roar of a lion; those who anger him forfeit their lives.
어 킹즈 래쓰 스트라익스 테어러 라익 더 로어 어브 어 라이언 도우즈 후 앵거 힘 포어핏 데어 라이브즈.
왕의 진노는 사자의 부르짖음 같으니 그를 노하게 하는 것은 자기의 생명을 해하는 것이니라

3 It is to one's honor to avoid strife, but every fool is quick to quarrel.
잇 이즈 투 원즈 아너 투 어보이드 스트라이프, 벗 에브리 풀 이즈 퀵 투 쿼럴.
다툼을 멀리 하는 것이 사람에게 영광이거늘 미련한 자마다 다툼을 일으키느니라

4 sluggards do not plow in season; so at harvest time they look but find nothing.
슬러거즈 두 낫 플라우 인 시전 소우 앳 하아버스트 타임 데이 룩 벗 파인드 너씽.
게으른 자는 가을에 밭 갈지 아니하나니 그러므로 거둘 때에는 구걸할지라도 얻지 못하리라

5 The purposes of a person's heart are deep waters, but one who has insight draws them out.
더 퍼퍼서즈 어브 어 퍼선즈 하아트 아아 딥 워터즈, 벗 원 후 해즈 인사이트 드로즈 뎀 아웃.
사람의 마음에 있는 모략은 깊은 물 같으니라 그럴지라도 명철한 사람은 그것을 길어 내느니라

6 Many claim to have unfailing love, but a faithful person who can find?
메니 클레임 투 해브 언페일링 러브, 벗 어 페이쓰펄 퍼선 후 캔 파인드?
많은 사람이 각기 자기의 인자함을 자랑하나니 충성된 자를 누가 만날 수 있으랴

7 The righteous lead blameless lives; blessed are their children after them.
더 라이처스 리드 블레임러스 라이브즈 블레스트 아아 데어 칠드런 애프터 뎀.
온전하게 행하는 자가 의인이라 그의 후손에게 복이 있느니라

8 When a king sits on his throne to judge, he winnows out all evil with his eyes.
웬 어 킹 싯스 안 히즈 쓰로운 투 저지, 히 위노우즈 아웃 올 이벌 윋 히즈 아이즈.
심판 자리에 앉은 왕은 그의 눈으로 모든 악을 흩어지게 하느니라

9 Who can say, "I have kept my heart pure; I am clean and without sin"?
후 캔 세이, 아이 해브 켑트 마이 하아트 퓨 아이 앰 클린 언드 위다우트 신?
내가 내 마음을 정하게 하였다 내 죄를 깨끗하게 하였다 할 자가 누구냐

10 Differing weights and differing measures—the LORD detests them both.

디퍼링 웨잇스 언드 디퍼링 메저즈 더 로어드 디테스트스 뎀 보우쓰.
한결같지 않은 저울 추와 한결같지 않은 되는 다 여호와께서 미워하시느니라
11 Even small children are known by their actions, so is their conduct really pure and upright?
이빈 스몰 칠드런 아아 노운 바이 데어 액션즈, 소우 이즈 데어 칸덕트 릴리 퓨 언드 업라이트?
비록 아이라도 자기의 동작으로 자기 품행이 청결한 여부와 정직한 여부를 나타내느니라
12 Ears that hear and eyes that see—the LORD has made them both.
이어즈 댓 히어 언드 아이즈 댓 시 더 로어드 해즈 메이드 뎀 보우쓰.
듣는 귀와 보는 눈은 다 여호와께서 지으신 것이니라
13 Do not love sleep or you will grow poor; stay awake and you will have food to spare.
두 낫 러브 슬립 오어 유 윌 그로우 푸어 스테이 어웨익 언드 유 윌 해브 푸드 투 스페어.
너는 잠자기를 좋아하지 말라 네가 빈궁하게 될까 두려우니라 네 눈을 뜨라 그리하면 양식이 족하리라
14 "It's no good, it's no good!" says the buyer—then goes off and boasts about the purchase.
잇스 노우 구드, 잇스 노우 구드! 세즈 더 바여 덴 고우즈 오프 언드 보우스트스 어바우트 더 퍼처스.
물건을 사는 자가 좋지 못하다 좋지 못하다 하다가 돌아간 후에는 자랑하느니라
15 Gold there is, and rubies in abundance, but lips that speak knowledge are a rare jewel.
고울드 데어 이즈, 언드 루비즈 인 어번던스, 벗 립스 댓 스픽 날러지 아아 어 레어 주얼.
세상에 금도 있고 진주도 많거니와 지혜로운 입술이 더욱 귀한 보배니라
16 Take the garment of one who puts up security for a stranger; hold it in pledge if it is done for an outsider.
테익 더 가아먼트 어브 원 후 풋스 업 시큐러티 포어 어 스트레인저 호울드 잇 인 플레지 이프 잇 이즈 던 포어 앤 아웃사이더.
타인을 위하여 보증 선 자의 옷을 취하라 외인들을 위하여 보증 선 자는 그의 몸을 볼모 잡을지니라
17 Food gained by fraud tastes sweet, but one ends up with a mouth full of gravel.
푸드 게인드 바이 프로드 테이스트스 스윗, 벗 원 엔즈 업 윋 어 마우쓰 풀 어브 그래벌.
속이고 취한 음식물은 사람에게 맛이 좋은 듯하나 후에는 그의 입에 모래가 가득하게 되리라
18 Plans are established by seeking advice; so if you wage war, obtain guidance.
플랜즈 아아 이스태블리쉬트 바이 시킹 애드바이스 소우 이프 유 웨이지 워어, 어브테인 가이던스.
경영은 의논함으로 성취하나니 지략을 베풀고 전쟁할지니라
19 A gossip betrays a confidence; so avoid anyone who talks too much.
어 가섭 빗레이즈 어 칸퍼덴스 소우 어보이드 에니원 후 톡스 투 머치.
두루 다니며 한담하는 자는 남의 비밀을 누설하나니 입술을 벌린 자를 사귀지 말지니라
20 If someone curses their father or mother, their lamp will be snuffed out in pitch darkness.
이프 서뭔 커시즈 데어 파더 오어 머더, 데어 램프 윌 비 스너프트 아웃 인 피치 다아크너스.
자기의 아비나 어미를 저주하는 자는 그의 등불이 흑암 중에 꺼짐을 당하리라
21 An inheritance claimed too soon will not be blessed at the end.
앤 인헤러턴스 클레임드 투 순 윌 낫 비 블레스트 앳 디 엔드.
처음에 속히 잡은 산업은 마침내 복이 되지 아니하느니라
22 Do not say, "I'll pay you back for this wrong!" Wait for the LORD, and he will avenge you.

두 낫 세이, 아일 페이 유 백 포어 디스 롱! 웨잇 포어 더 로어드, 언드 히 윌 어벤지 유.
너는 악을 갚겠다 말하지 말고 여호와를 기다리라 그가 너를 구원하시리라

23 The LORD detests differing weights, and dishonest scales do not please him.
더 로어드 디테스트스 디퍼링 웨잇스, 언드 디사너스트 스케일즈 두 낫 플리즈 힘.
한결같지 않은 저울 추는 여호와께서 미워하시는 것이요 속이는 저울은 좋지 못한 것이니라

24 A person's steps are directed by the LORD. How then can anyone understand their own way?
어 퍼선즈 스텝스 아아 더렉터드 바이 디 로어드. 하우 덴 캔 에니원 언더스탠드 데어 오운 웨이?
사람의 걸음은 여호와로 말미암나니 사람이 어찌 자기의 길을 알 수 있으랴

25 It is a trap to dedicate something rashly and only later to consider one's vows.
잇 이즈 어 트랩 투 데더케이트 섬씽 래슬리 언드 오운리 레이터 투 컨시더 원즈 바우즈.
함부로 이 물건은 거룩하다 하여 서원하고 그 후에 살피면 그것이 그 사람에게 덫이 되느니라

26 A wise king winnows out the wicked; he drives the threshing wheel over them.
어 와이즈 킹 위노우즈 아웃 더 위커드 히 드라이브즈 더 쓰레쉉 윌 오우버 뎀.
지혜로운 왕은 악인들을 키질하며 타작하는 바퀴를 그들 위에 굴리느니라

27 The human spirit is the lamp of the LORD that sheds light on one's inmost being.
더 휴먼 스피릿 이즈 더 램프 어브 더 로어드 댓 셰즈 라이트 안 원즈 인모우스트 비잉.
사람의 영혼은 여호와의 등불이라 사람의 깊은 속을 살피느니라

28 Love and faithfulness keep a king safe; through love his throne is made secure.
러브 언드 페이쓰펄네스 킵 어 킹 세이프 쓰루 러브 히즈 쓰로운 이즈 메이드 시큐.
왕은 인자와 진리로 스스로 보호하고 그의 왕위도 인자함으로 말미암아 견고하니라

29 The glory of young men is their strength, gray hair the splendor of the old.
더 글로어리 어브 영 멘 이즈 데어 스트렝쓰, 그레이 헤어 더 스플렌더 어브 디 오울드.
젊은 자의 영화는 그의 힘이요 늙은 자의 아름다움은 백발이니라

30 Blows and wounds scrub away evil, and beatings purge the inmost being.
블로우즈 언드 원즈스 크러브 어웨이 이벌, 언드 비팅즈 퍼지 디 인모우스트 비잉.
상하게 때리는 것이 악을 없이하나니 매는 사람 속에 깊이 들어가느니라

beer [biər] n. 맥주
terror [térər] n. 공포, 두려움
roar [rɔːr] vi. 으르렁거리다
lion [láiən] n. 사자
plow [plau] n. 쟁기
season [síːzən] n. 계절
purpose [pə́ːrpəs] n. 목적
draw [drɔː] vt. 끌다
king [kiŋ] n. 왕, 국왕
clean [kliːn] a. 청결한
measure [méʒər] vt. 재다
both [bouθ] a. 양쪽의, 쌍방의
small [smɔːl] a. 작은, 소형의
action [ǽkʃən] n. 활동, 행동
conduct [kɑ́ndʌkt] n. 행위
really [ríːəli] ad. 참으로
boast [boust] vi. 자랑하다
purchase [pə́ːrtʃəs] vt. 사다
gravel [grǽvəl] n. 자갈
claim [kleim] vt. 요구하다
winnow [wínou] vt. 까부르다
thresh [θreʃ] vt. 타작하다
pitch [pitʃ] vt. 던지다
splendor [spléndər] n. 빛남, 광휘

21장 1 In the LORD's hand the king's heart is a stream of water that he channels toward all who please him.
인 더 로어즈 핸드 더 킹즈 하아트 이즈 어 스트림 어브 워터 댓 히 채널즈 터워어드 올 후 플리즈 힘.
왕의 마음이 여호와의 손에 있음이 마치 봇물과 같아서 그가 임의로 인도하시느니라

2 A person may think their own ways are right, but the LORD weighs the heart.

어 퍼선 메이 씽크 데어 오운 웨이즈 아아 라이트, 벗 더 로어드 웨이즈 더 하아트.
사람의 행위가 자기 보기에는 모두 정직하여도 여호와는 마음을 감찰하시느니라

3 To do what is right and just is more acceptable to the LORD than sacrifice.
투 두 웟 이즈 라이트 언드 저스트 이즈 모어 액셉터벌 투 더 로어드 던 새크러파이스.
공의와 정의를 행하는 것은 제사 드리는 것보다 여호와께서 기쁘게 여기시느니라

4 Haughty eyes and a proud heart—the unplowed field of the wicked—produce sin.
호티 아이즈 언드 어 프라우드 하아트 디 언플라우드 필드 어브 더 위커드 프로우두스 신.
눈이 높은 것과 마음이 교만한 것과 악인이 형통한 것은 다 죄니라

5 The plans of the diligent lead to profit as surely as haste leads to poverty.
더 플랜즈 어브 더 딜리전트 리드 투 프라펏 애즈 슈얼리 애즈 헤이스트 리즈 투 파버티.
부지런한 자의 경영은 풍부함에 이를 것이나 조급한 자는 궁핍함에 이를 따름이니라

6 A fortune made by a lying tongue is a fleeting vapor and a deadly snare.
어 포어천 메이드 바이 어 라이잉 텅 이즈 어 플리팅 베이퍼 언드 어 데들리 스네어.
속이는 말로 재물을 모으는 것은 죽음을 구하는 것이라 곧 불려다니는 안개니라

7 The violence of the wicked will drag them away, for they refuse to do what is right.
더 바이얼런스 어브 더 위커드 윌 드래그 뎀 어웨이, 포어 데이 레퓨즈 투 두 웟 이즈 라이트.
악인의 강포는 자기를 소멸하나니 이는 정의를 행하기 싫어함이니라

8 The way of the guilty is devious, but the conduct of the innocent is upright.
더 웨이 어브 더 길티 이즈 디비어스, 벗 더 칸덕트 어브 디 이너선트 이즈 업라이트.
죄를 크게 범한 자의 길은 심히 구부러지고 깨끗한 자의 길은 곧으니라

9 Better to live on a corner of the roof than share a house with a quarrelsome wife.
베터 투 리브 안 어 코어너 어브 더 루프 던 셰어 어 하우스 윋 어 쿼럴섬 와이프.
다투는 여인과 함께 큰 집에서 사는 것보다 움막에서 사는 것이 나으니라

10 The wicked crave evil; their neighbors get no mercy from them.
더 위커드 크레이브 이벌 데어 네이버즈 겟 노우 머시 프럼 뎀.
악인의 마음은 남의 재앙을 원하나니 그 이웃도 그 앞에서 은혜를 입지 못하느니라

11 When a mocker is punished, the simple gain wisdom; by paying attention to the wise they get knowledge.
웬 어 마커 이즈 퍼니쉬트, 더 심펄 게인 위즈덤 바이 페이잉 어텐션 투 더 와이즈 데이 겟 날러지.
거만한 자가 벌을 받으면 어리석은 자도 지혜를 얻겠고 지혜로운 자가 교훈을 받으면 지식이 더하리라

12 The Righteous One takes note of the house of the wicked and brings the wicked to ruin.
더 라이처스 원 테익스 노우트 어브 더 하우스 어브 더 위커드 언드 브링즈 더 위커드 투 루언.
의로우신 자는 악인의 집을 감찰하시고 악인을 환난에 던지시느니라

13 Whoever shuts their ears to the cry of the poor will also cry out and not be answered.
후에버 셧스 데어 이어즈 투 더 크라이 어브 더 푸어 윌 올소우 크라이 아웃 언드 낫 비 앤서드.
귀를 막고 가난한 자가 부르짖는 소리를 듣지 아니하면 자기가 부르짖을 때에도 들을 자가 없으리라

14 A gift given in secret soothes anger, and a bribe concealed in the cloak pacifies great wrath.
어 기프트 기번 인 시크럿 숟즈 앵거, 언드 어 브라이브 컨실드 인 더 클로욱 패서파이즈 그레이트 래쓰.

은밀한 선물은 노를 쉬게 하고 품 안의 뇌물은 맹렬한 분을 그치게 하느니라

15 When justice is done, it brings joy to the righteous but terror to evildoers.
웬 저스터스 이즈 던, 잇 브링즈 조이 투 더 라이처스 벗 테어러 투 이벌두어즈.
정의를 행하는 것이 의인에게는 즐거움이요 죄인에게는 패망이니라

16 Whoever strays from the path of prudence comes to rest in the company of the dead.
후에버 스트레이즈 프럼 더 패쓰 어브 프루던스 컴즈 투 레스트 인 더 컴퍼니 어브 더 데드.
명철의 길을 떠난 사람은 사망의 회중에 거하리라

17 Whoever loves pleasure will become poor; whoever loves wine and olive oil will never be rich.
후에버 러브즈 플레저 윌 비컴 푸어 후에버 러브즈 와인 언드 알러브 오일 윌 네버 비 리치.
연락을 좋아하는 자는 가난하게 되고 술과 기름을 좋아하는 자는 부하게 되지 못하느니라

18 The wicked become a ransom for the righteous, and the unfaithful for the upright.
더 위커드 비컴 어 랜섬 포어 더 라이처스, 언드 디 언페이쓰펄 포어 디 업라이트.
악인은 의인의 속전이 되고 사악한 자는 정직한 자의 대신이 되느니라

19 Better to live in a desert than with a quarrelsome and nagging wife.
베터 투 리브 인 어 데저트 던 윋 어 쿼럴섬 언드 내깅 와이프.
다투며 성내는 여인과 함께 사는 것보다 광야에서 사는 것이 나으니라

20 The wise store up choice food and olive oil, but fools gulp theirs down.
더 와이즈 스토어 업 초이스 푸드 언드 알러브 오일, 벗 풀즈 걸프 데어즈 다운.
지혜 있는 자의 집에는 귀한 보배와 기름이 있으나 미련한 자는 이것을 다 삼켜 버리느니라

21 Whoever pursues righteousness and love finds life, prosperity and honor.
후에버 퍼수즈 라이처스너스 언드 러브 파인즈 라이프, 프라스페러티 언드 아너.
공의와 인자를 따라 구하는 자는 생명과 공의와 영광을 얻느니라

22 One who is wise can go up against the city of the mighty and pull down the stronghold in which they trust.
원 후 이즈 와이즈 캔 고우 업 어겐스트 더 시티 어브 더 마이티 언드 풀 다운 더 스트롱호울드 인 위치 데이 트러스트.
지혜로운 자는 용사의 성에 올라가서 그 성이 의지하는 방벽을 허느니라

23 Those who guard their mouths and their tongues keep themselves from calamity.
도우즈 후 가아드 데어 마욷즈 언드 데어 텅즈 킵 뎀셀브즈 프럼 컬래머티.
입과 혀를 지키는 자는 자기의 영혼을 환난에서 보전하느니라

24 The proud and arrogant person—"Mocker" is his name—behaves with insolent fury.
더 프라우드 언드 에어러건트 퍼선 마커 이즈 히즈 네임 비헤이브즈 윋 인설런트 퓨리.
무례하고 교만한 자를 이름하여 망령된 자라 하나니 이는 넘치는 교만으로 행함이니라

25 The craving of a sluggard will be the death of him, because his hands refuse to work.
더 크레이빙 어브 어 슬러거드 윌 비 더 데쓰 어브 힘, 비카즈 히즈 핸즈 레퓨즈 투 웍.
게으른 자의 욕망이 자기를 죽이나니 이는 자기의 손으로 일하기를 싫어함이니라

26 All day long he craves for more, but the righteous give without sparing.
올 데이 롱 히 크레이브즈 포어 모어, 벗 더 라이처스 기브 위다우트 스페링.

어떤 자는 종일토록 탐하기만 하나 의인은 아끼지 아니하고 베푸느니라

27 The sacrifice of the wicked is detestable—how much more so when brought with evil intent!
더 새크러파이스 어브 더 위커드 이즈 디테스터벌 하우 머치 모어 소우 웬 브룻 윋 이벌 인텐트!
악인의 제물은 본래 가증하거든 하물며 악한 뜻으로 드리는 것이랴

28 A false witness will perish, but a careful listener will testify successfully.
어 폴스 윗너스 윌 페어리쉬, 벗 어 케어펄 리서너 윌 테스티파이 석세스펄리.
거짓 증인은 패망하려니와 확실히 들은 사람의 말은 힘이 있느니라

29 The wicked put up a bold front, but the upright give thought to their ways.
더 위커드 풋 업 어 보울드 프런트, 벗 디 업라이트 기브 쏫 투 데어 웨이즈.
악인은 자기의 얼굴을 굳게 하나 정직한 자는 자기의 행위를 삼가느니라

30 There is no wisdom, no insight, no plan that can succeed against the LORD.
데어 이즈 노우 위즈덤, 노우 인사이트, 노우 플랜 댓 캔 석시드 어겐스트 더 로어드.
지혜로도 못하고, 명철로도 못하고 모략으로도 여호와를 당하지 못하느니라

31 The horse is made ready for the day of battle, but victory rests with the LORD.
더 호어스 이즈 메이드 레디 포어 더 데이 어브 배털, 벗 빅터어리 레스트스 윋 더 로어드.
싸울 날을 위하여 마병을 예비하거니와 이김은 여호와께 있느니라

channel [tʃǽnl] n. 해협, 수로
toward [tɔːrd] prep. …쪽으로
may [mei] v. …할지도 모른다
think [θiŋk] vt. …라고 여기다
field [fiːld] n. 들, 벌판
surely [ʃúərli] ad. 확실히
fortune [fɔ́ːrtʃən] n. 운, 우연
vapor [véipər] n. 증기, 수증기

crave [kreiv] vt. 열망하다
mercy [mə́ːrsi] n. 자비, 연민
note [nout] n. 각서, 비망록
refuse [rifjúːz] vt. 거절하다
soothe [suːð] vt. 달래다
cloak [klouk] n. 외투
insolent [ínsələnt] a. 무례한
fury [fjúəri] n. 격노, 격분

shut [ʃʌt] vt. 닫다
ear [iər] n. 귀
cry [krai] vi. 소리치다
also [ɔ́ːlsou] ad. …도 또한
careful [kέərfəl] a. 주의 깊은
great [greit] a. 큰, 거대한
mighty [máiti] a. 강력한
battle [bǽtl] n. 전투

22장 1 A good name is more desirable than great riches; to be esteemed is better than silver or gold.
어 구드 네임 이즈 모어 디자이러벌 던 그레이트 리처즈 투 비 에스팀드 이즈 베터 던 실버 오어 고울드.
많은 재물보다 명예를 택할 것이요 은이나 금보다 은총을 더욱 택할 것이니라

2 Rich and poor have this in common: The LORD is the Maker of them all.
리치 언드 푸어 해브 디스 인 카먼 더 로어드 이즈 더 메이커 어브 뎀 올.
가난한 자와 부한 자가 함께 살거니와 그 모두를 지으신 이는 여호와시니라

3 The prudent see danger and take refuge, but the simple keep going and pay the penalty.
더 프루던트 시 데인저 언드 테익 레퓨지, 벗 더 심펄 킵 고우잉 언드 페이 더 페널티.
슬기로운 자는 재앙을 보면 숨어 피하여도 어리석은 자는 나가다가 해를 받느니라

4 Humility is the fear of the LORD; its wages are riches and honor and life.
휴밀리티 이즈 더 피어 어브 더 로어드 잇 스웨이저즈 아아 리처즈 언드 아너 언드 라이프.
겸손과 여호와를 경외함의 보상은 재물과 영광과 생명이니라

5 In the paths of the wicked are snares and pitfalls, but those who would preserve their life stay far from them.

인 더 팬즈 어브 더 위커드 아아 스네어즈 언드 핏폴즈, 벗 도우즈 후 워드 프러저브 데어 라이프 스테이 파아 프럼 뎀.

패역한 자의 길에는 가시와 올무가 있거니와 영혼을 지키는 자는 이를 멀리 하느니라

6 Start children off on the way they should go, and even when they are old they will not turn from it.

스타아트 칠드런 오프 안 더 웨이 데이 슈드 고우, 언드 이빈 웬 데이 아아 오울드 데이 윌 낫 턴 프럼 잇.

마땅히 행할 길을 아이에게 가르치라 그리하면 늙어도 그것을 떠나지 아니하리라

7 The rich rule over the poor, and the borrower is slave to the lender.

더 리치 룰 오우버 더 푸어, 언드 더 바아로우어 이즈 슬레이브 투 더 렌더.

부자는 가난한 자를 주관하고 빚진 자는 채주의 종이 되느니라

8 Whoever sows injustice reaps calamity, and the rod they wield in fury will be broken.

후에버 소우즈 인저스티스 립스 컬래머티, 언드 더 라드 데이 윌드 인 퓨리 윌 비 브로우컨.

악을 뿌리는 자는 재앙을 거두리니 그 분노의 기세가 쇠하리라

9 The generous will themselves be blessed, for they share their food with the poor.

더 제너러스 윌 뎀셀브즈 비 블레스트, 포어 데이 셰어 데어 푸드 윋 더 푸어.

선한 눈을 가진 자는 복을 받으리니 이는 양식을 가난한 자에게 줌이니라

10 Drive out the mocker, and out goes strife; quarrels and insults are ended.

드라이브 아웃 더 마커, 언드 아웃 고우즈 스트라이프 쿼럴즈 언드 인설트스 아아 엔더드.

거만한 자를 쫓아내면 다툼이 쉬고 싸움과 수욕이 그치느니라

11 One who loves a pure heart and who speaks with grace will have the king for a friend.

원 후 러브즈 어 퓨 하아트 언드 후 스픽스 윋 그레이스 윌 해브 더 킹 포어 어 프렌드.

마음의 정결을 사모하는 자의 입술에는 덕이 있으므로 임금이 그의 친구가 되느니라

12 The eyes of the LORD keep watch over knowledge, but he frustrates the words of the unfaithful.

디 아이즈 어브 더 로어드 킵 와치 오우버 날러지, 벗 히 프러스트레잇스 더 워즈 어브 디 언페이쓰펄.

여호와의 눈은 지식 있는 사람을 지키시나 사악한 사람의 말은 패하게 하시느니라

13 The sluggard says, "There's a lion outside! I'll be killed in the public square!"

더 슬러거드 세즈, 데어즈 어 라이언 아웃사이드! 아일 비 킬드 인 더 퍼블릭 스퀘!

게으른 자는 말하기를 사자가 밖에 있은즉 내가 나가면 거리에서 찢기겠다 하느니라

14 The mouth of an adulteress woman is a deep pit; a man who is under the LORD's wrath falls into it.

더 마우쓰 어브 앤 어덜터레스 워먼 이즈 어 딥 핏 어 맨 후 이즈 언더 더 로어즈 래쓰 폴즈 인투 잇.

음녀의 입은 깊은 함정이라 여호와의 노를 당한 자는 거기 빠지리라

15 Folly is bound up in the heart of a child, but the rod of discipline will drive it far away.

팔리 이즈 바운드 업 인 더 하아트 어브 어 차일드, 벗 더 라드 어브 디서플린 윌 드라이브 잇 파아 어웨이.

아이의 마음에는 미련한 것이 얽혔으나 징계하는 채찍이 이를 멀리 쫓아내리라

16 One who oppresses the poor to increase his wealth and one who gives gifts to the rich—both come to poverty.

원 후 업레시즈 더 푸어 투 인크리스 히즈 웰쓰 언드 원 후 기브즈 기프트스 투 더 리치 보우쓰 컴 투 파버티.

이익을 얻으려고 가난한 자를 학대하는 자와 부자에게 주는 자는 가난하여질 뿐이니라

17 Pay attention and turn your ear to the sayings of the wise; apply your heart to what I teach,

페이 어텐션 언드 턴 요어 이어 투 더 세이잉즈 어브 더 와이즈 업라이 요어 하아트 투 웟 아이 티치.
너는 귀를 기울여 지혜 있는 자의 말씀을 들으며 내 지식에 마음을 둘지어다

18 for it is pleasing when you keep them in your heart and have all of them ready on your lips.
포어 잇 이즈 플리징 웬 유 킵 뎀 인 요어 하아트 언드 해브 올 어브 뎀 레디 안 요어 립스.
이것을 네 속에 보존하며 네 입술 위에 함께 있게 함이 아름다우니라

19 So that your trust may be in the LORD, I teach you today, even you.
소우 댓 요어 트러스트 메이 비 인 더 로어드, 아이 티치 유 터데이, 이빈 유.
내가 네게 여호와를 의뢰하게 하려 하여 이것을 오늘 특별히 네게 알게 하였노니

20 Have I not written thirty sayings for you, sayings of counsel and knowledge,
해브 아이 낫 리턴 써디 세이잉즈 포어 유, 세이잉즈 어브 카운설 언드 날러지.
내가 모략과 지식의 아름다운 것을 너를 위해 기록하여

21 teaching you to be honest and to speak the truth, so that you bring back truthful reports to those you serve?
티칭 유 투 비 아너스트 언드 투 스픽 더 트루쓰, 소우 댓 유 브링 백 트루쓰펄 리포어트스 투 도우즈 유 서브?
네가 진리의 확실한 말씀을 깨닫게 하며 또 너를 보내는 자에게 진리의 말씀으로 회답하게 하려 함이 아니냐

22 Do not exploit the poor because they are poor and do not crush the needy in court,
두 낫 엑스플로이트 더 푸어 비카즈 데이 아아 푸어 언드 두 낫 크러쉬 더 니디 인 코어트,
약한 자를 그가 약하다고 탈취하지 말며 곤고한 자를 성문에서 압제하지 말라

23 for the LORD will take up their case and will exact life for life.
포어 더 로어드 윌 테익 업 데어 케이스 언드 윌 이그잭트 라이프 포어 라이프.
대저 여호와께서 신원하여 주시고 또 그를 노략하는 자의 생명을 빼앗으시리라

24 Do not make friends with a hot-tempered person, do not associate with one easily angered,
두 낫 메익 프렌즈 윋 어 핫템퍼드 퍼선, 두 낫 어소우시엇 윋 원 이절리 앵거드.
노를 품는 자와 사귀지 말며 울분한 자와 동행하지 말지니

25 or you may learn their ways and get yourself ensnared.
오어 유 메이 런 데어 웨이즈 언드 겟 요어셀프 인스네어드.
그의 행위를 본받아 네 영혼을 올무에 빠뜨릴까 두려움이니라

26 Do not be one who shakes hands in pledge or puts up security for debts;
두 낫 비 원 후 셰익스 핸즈 인 플레지 오어 풋스 업 시큐러티 포어 뎃스
너는 사람과 더불어 손을 잡지 말며 남의 빚에 보증을 서지 말라

27 if you lack the means to pay, your very bed will be snatched from under you.
이프 유 랙 더 민즈 투 페이, 요어 베어리 베드 윌 비 스내치트 프럼 언더 유.
만일 갚을 것이 네게 없으면 네 누운 침상도 빼앗길 것이라 네가 어찌 그리하겠느냐

28 Do not move an ancient boundary stone set up by your ancestors.
두 낫 무브 앤 에인션트 바운더리 스토운 셋 업 바이 요어 앤세스터즈.
네 선조가 세운 옛 지계석을 옮기지 말지니라

29 Do you see someone skilled in their work? They will serve before kings; they will not serve before officials of low rank.

두 유 시 서뮌 스킬드 인 데어 웍? 데이 윌 서브 비포어 킹즈 데이 윌 낫 서브 비포어 어피셜즈 어브 로우 랭크.
네가 자기의 일에 능숙한 사람을 보았느냐 이러한 사람은 왕 앞에 설 것이요 천한 자 앞에 서지 아니하리라

desirable [dizáiərəbəl] a. 바람직한
esteem [istíːm] vt. 존경하다
common [kάmən] a. 공통의
all [ɔːl] a. 모든, 전부의
danger [déindʒər] n. 위험
refuge [réfjuːdʒ] n. 피난, 보호
penalty [pénəlti] n. 형, 형벌
far [fɑːr] ad. 멀리
old [ould] a. 나이 먹은, 늙은
turn [təːrn] vt. 돌리다
borrow [bɔ́(ː)rou] vt. 빌리다
lend [lend] vt. 빌리다
wield [wiːld] vt. 휘두르다
generous [dʒénərəs] a. 후한
drive [draiv] vt. 몰다, 쫓다
ready [rédi] a. 준비가 된
trust [trʌst] n. 신뢰
truth [truːθ] n. 진리, 참
exploit [iksplɔ́it] vt. 착취하다
court [kɔːrt] n. 안뜰, 뜰
debt [det] n. 빚, 부채
ancestor [ǽnsestər] n. 선조
case [keis] n. 경우, 사례
exact [igzǽkt] a. 정확한

23장 1 When you sit to dine with a ruler, note well what is before you,
웬 유 싯 투 다인 윋 어 룰러, 노우트 웰 웟 이즈 비포어 유.
네가 관원과 함께 앉아 음식을 먹게 되거든 삼가 네 앞에 있는 자가 누구인지를 생각하며

2 and put a knife to your throat if you are given to gluttony.
언드 풋 어 나이프 투 요어 쓰로우트 이프 유 아아 기번 투 글러터니.
네가 만일 음식을 탐하는 자이거든 네 목에 칼을 둘 것이니라

3 Do not crave his delicacies, for that food is deceptive.
두 낫 크레이브 히즈 델리커시즈, 포어 댓 푸드 이즈 디셉티브.
그의 맛있는 음식을 탐하지 말라 그것은 속이는 음식이니라

4 Do not wear yourself out to get rich; do not trust your own cleverness.
두 낫 웨어 요어셀프 아웃 투 겟 리치 두 낫 트러스트 요어 오운 클레버너스.
부자 되기에 애쓰지 말고 네 사사로운 지혜를 버릴지어다

5 Cast but a glance at riches, and they are gone, for they will surely sprout wings and fly off to the sky like an eagle.
캐스트 벗 어 글랜스 앳 리처즈, 언드 데이 아아 곤, 포어 데이 윌 슈얼리 스프라우트 윙즈 언드 플라이 오프 투 더 스카이 라익 앤 이걸.
네가 어찌 허무한 것에 주목하겠느냐 정녕히 재물은 스스로 날개를 내어 하늘을 나는 독수리처럼 날아가리라

6 Do not eat the food of a begrudging host, do not crave his delicacies;
두 낫 잇 더 푸드 어브 어 비그러징 호우스트, 두 낫 크레이브 히즈 델리커시즈
악한 눈이 있는 자의 음식을 먹지 말며 그의 맛있는 음식을 탐하지 말지어다

7 for he is the kind of person who is always thinking about the cost. "Eat and drink," he says to you, but his heart is not with you.
포어 히 이즈 더 카인드 어브 퍼선 후 이즈 올웨이즈 씽킹 어바우트 더 카스트. 잇 언드 드링크, 히 세즈 투 유, 벗 히즈 하아트 이즈 낫 윋 유.
대저 그 마음의 생각이 어떠하면 그 위인도 그러한즉 그가 네게 먹고 마시라 할지라도 그의 마음은 너와 함께 하지 아니함이라

8 You will vomit up the little you have eaten and will have wasted your compliments.
유 윌 바멋 업 더 리털 유 해브 이턴 언드 윌 해브 웨이스터드 요어 캄플러멘트스.

네가 조금 먹은 것도 토하겠고 네 아름다운 말도 헛된 데로 돌아가리라

9 Do not speak to fools, for they will scorn your prudent words.
두 낫 스픽 투 풀즈, 포어 데이 윌 스콘 요어 프루던트 워즈.
미련한 자의 귀에 말하지 말지니 이는 그가 네 지혜로운 말을 업신여길 것임이니라

10 Do not move an ancient boundary stone or encroach on the fields of the fatherless,
두 낫 무브 앤 에인션트 바운더리 스토운 오어 인크로우치 안 더 필즈 어브 더 파덜러스.
옛 지계석을 옮기지 말며 고아들의 밭을 침범하지 말지어다

11 for their Defender is strong; he will take up their case against you.
포어 데어 디펜더 이즈 스트롱 히 윌 테익 업 데어 케이스 어겐스트 유.
대저 그들의 구속자는 강하시니 그가 너를 대적하여 그들의 원한을 풀어 주시리라

12 Apply your heart to instruction and your ears to words of knowledge.
업라이 요어 하아트 투 인스트럭션 언드 요어 이어즈 투 워즈 어브 날러지.
훈계에 착심하며 지식의 말씀에 귀를 기울이라

13 Do not withhold discipline from a child; if you punish them with the rod, they will not die.
두 낫 위쓰호울드 디서플런 프럼 어 차일드 이프 유 퍼니쉬 뎀 윋 더 라드, 데이 윌 낫 다이.
아이를 훈계하지 아니하려고 하지 말라 채찍으로 그를 때릴지라도 그가 죽지 아니하리라

14 Punish them with the rod and save them from death.
퍼니쉬 뎀 윋 더 라드 언드 세이브 뎀 프럼 데쓰.
네가 그를 채찍으로 때리면 그의 영혼을 스올에서 구원하리라

15 My son, if your heart is wise, then my heart will be glad indeed;
마이 선, 이프 요어 하아트 이즈 와이즈, 덴 마이 하아트 윌 비 글래드 인디드
내 아들아 만일 네 마음이 지혜로우면 나 곧 내 마음이 즐겁겠고

16 my inmost being will rejoice when your lips speak what is right.
마이 인모우스트 비잉 윌 리조이스 웬 요어 립스 스픽 윗 이즈 라이트.
만일 네 입술이 정직을 말하면 내 속이 유쾌하리라

17 Do not let your heart envy sinners, but always be zealous for the fear of the LORD.
두 낫 렛 요어 하아트 엔비 시너즈, 벗 올 웨이즈 비 젤러스 포어 더 피어 어브 더 로어드.
네 마음으로 죄인의 형통을 부러워하지 말고 항상 여호와를 경외하라

18 There is surely a future hope for you, and your hope will not be cut off.
데어 이즈 슈얼리 어 퓨처 호웁 포어 유, 언드 요어 호웁 윌 낫 비 컷 오프.
정녕히 네 장래가 있겠고 네 소망이 끊어지지 아니하리라

19 Listen, my son, and be wise, and set your heart on the right path:
리선, 마이 선, 언드 비 와이즈, 언드 셋 요어 하아트 안 더 라이트 패쓰
내 아들아 너는 듣고 지혜를 얻어 네 마음을 바른 길로 인도할지니라

20 Do not join those who drink too much wine or gorge themselves on meat,
두 낫 조인 도우즈 후 드링크 투 머치 와인 오어 고어지 뎀셀브즈 안 밋.
술을 즐겨 하는 자들과 고기를 탐하는 자들과도 더불어 사귀지 말라

21 for drunkards and gluttons become poor, and drowsiness clothes them in rags.

포어 드렁커즈 언드 글러턴즈 비컴 푸어, 언드 드라우지너스 클로욷즈 뎀 인 래그즈.

술 취하고 음식을 탐하는 자는 가난하여질 것이요 잠 자기를 즐겨 하는 자는 해어진 옷을 입을 것임이니라

22 Listen to your father, who gave you life, and do not despise your mother when she is old.

리선 투 요어 파더, 후 게이브 유 라이프, 언드 두 낫 디스파이즈 요어 머더 웬 쉬 이즈 오울드.

너를 낳은 아비에게 청종하고 네 늙은 어미를 경히 여기지 말지니라

23 Buy the truth and do not sell it—wisdom, instruction and insight as well.

바이 더 트루쓰 언드 두 낫 셀 잇 위즈덤, 인스트럭션 언드 인사이트 애즈 웰.

진리를 사되 팔지는 말며 지혜와 훈계와 명철도 그리할지니라

24 The father of a righteous child has great joy; a man who fathers a wise son rejoices in him.

더 파더 어브 어 라이처스 차일드 해즈 그레이트 조이 어 맨 후 파더즈 어 와이즈 선 리조이서즈 인 힘.

의인의 아비는 크게 즐거울 것이요 지혜로운 자식을 낳은 자는 그로 말미암아 즐거울 것이니라

25 May your father and mother rejoice; may she who gave you birth be joyful!

메이 요어 파더 언드 머더 리조이스 메이 쉬 후 게이브 유 버쓰 비 조이펄!

네 부모를 즐겁게 하며 너를 낳은 어미를 기쁘게 하라

26 My son, give me your heart and let your eyes delight in my ways,

마이 선, 기브 미 요어 하아트 언드 렛 요어 아이즈 딜랏 인 마이 웨이즈.

내 아들아 네 마음을 내게 주며 네 눈으로 내 길을 즐거워할지어다

27 for an adulterous woman is a deep pit, and a wayward wife is a narrow well.

포어 앤 어덜터러스 워먼 이즈 어 딥 핏, 언드 어 웨이워드 와이프 이즈 어 네어로우 웰.

대저 음녀는 깊은 구덩이요 이방 여인은 좁은 함정이라

28 Like a bandit she lies in wait and multiplies the unfaithful among men.

라익 어 밴딧 쉬 라이즈 인 웨잇 언드 멀터플라이즈 디 언페이쓰펄 어멍 멘.

참으로 그는 강도 같이 매복하며 사람들 중에 사악한 자가 많아지게 하느니라

29 Who has woe? Who has sorrow? Who has strife? Who has complaints? Who has needless bruises? Who has bloodshot eyes?

후 해즈 워우? 후 해즈 사아로우? 후 해즈 스트라이프? 후 해즈 컴플레인트스? 후 해즈 니들러스 브루저즈? 후 해즈 블러드샷 아이즈?

재앙이 뉘게 있느뇨 근심이 뉘게 있느뇨 분쟁이 뉘게 있느뇨 원망이 뉘게 있느뇨 까닭 없는 상처가 뉘게 있느뇨 붉은 눈이 뉘게 있느뇨

30 Those who linger over wine, who go to sample bowls of mixed wine.

도우즈 후 링거 오우버 와인, 후 고우 투 샘펄 보울즈 어브 믹스트 와인.

술에 잠긴 자에게 있고 혼합한 술을 구하러 다니는 자에게 있느니라

31 Do not gaze at wine when it is red, when it sparkles in the cup, when it goes down smoothly!

두 낫 게이즈 앳 와인 웬 잇 이즈 레드, 웬 잇 스파아컬즈 인 더 컵, 웬 잇 고우즈 다운 스무들리!

포도주는 붉고 잔에서 번쩍이며 순하게 내려가나니 너는 그것을 보지도 말지어다

32 In the end it bites like a snake and poisons like a viper.

인 디 엔드 잇 바잇스 라익 어 스네익 언드 포이전즈 라익 어 바이퍼.

그것이 마침내 뱀 같이 물 것이요 독사 같이 쏠 것이며

33 Your eyes will see strange sights, and your mind will imagine confusing things.
요어 아이즈 윌 시 스트레인지 사잇스, 언드 요어 마인드 윌 이매전 컨퓨징 씽즈.
또 네 눈에는 괴이한 것이 보일 것이요 네 마음은 구부러진 말을 할 것이며

34 You will be like one sleeping on the high seas, lying on top of the rigging.
유 윌 비 라익 원 슬리핑 안 더 하이 시즈, 라이잉 안 탑 어브 더 리깅.
너는 바다 가운데에 누운 자 같을 것이요 돛대 위에 누운 자 같을 것이며

35 "They hit me," you will say, "but I'm not hurt! They beat me, but I don't feel it! When will I wake up so I can find another drink?"
데이 힛 미, 유 윌 세이, 벗 아임 낫 허트! 데이 빗 미, 벗 아이 도운트 필 잇! 웬 윌 아이 웨익 업 소우 아이 캔 파인드 어너더 드링크?
네가 스스로 말하기를 사람이 나를 때려도 나는 아프지 아니하고 나를 상하게 하여도 내게 감각이 없도다 내가 언제나 깰까 다시 술을 찾겠다 하리라

dine [dain] vi. 정찬을 들다	begrudge [bigrʌ́dʒ] vt. 시기하다	inmost [ínmòust] a. 맨 안쪽의
note [nout] n. 주목, 주의	host [houst] n. 주인	envy [énvi] n. 질투, 부러움
throat [θrout] n. 목, 인후	thinking [θíŋkiŋ] a. 생각하는	zealous [zéləs] a. 열심인
gluttony [glʌ́təni] n. 대식	vomit [vámit] vi. 토하다	drunkard [drʌ́ŋkərd] n. 술고래
delicacy [délikəsi] n. 섬세	waste [weist] vt. 헛되이 하다	rag [ræg] n. 넝마
cleverness [klévərnis] n. 영리함	compliment [kámpləmənt] n. 경의	bandit [bǽndit] n. 산적
glance [glæns] n. 흘긋 봄, 일별	encroach [enkróutʃ] vi. 침입하다	rigging [ríɡiŋ] n. 의장
sprout [spraut] vi. 싹이 트다	defender [diféndər] n. 방어자	gaze [geiz] n. 응시, 주시

24장 1 Do not envy the wicked, do not desire their company;
두 낫 엔비 더 위커드, 두 낫 디자여 데어 컴퍼니
너는 악인의 형통함을 부러워하지 말며 그와 함께 있으려고 하지도 말지어다

2 for their hearts plot violence, and their lips talk about making trouble.
포어 데어 하아트스 플랏 바이얼런스, 언드 데어 립스 톡 어바우트 메이킹 트러벌.
그들의 마음은 강포를 품고 그들의 입술은 재앙을 말함이니라

3 By wisdom a house is built, and through understanding it is established;
바이 위즈덤 어 하우스 이즈 빌트, 언드 쓰루 언더스탠딩 잇 이즈 이스태블리쉬트
집은 지혜로 말미암아 건축되고 명철로 말미암아 견고하게 되며

4 through knowledge its rooms are filled with rare and beautiful treasures.
쓰루 날러지 잇스 룸즈 아아 필드 윋 레어 언드 뷰터펄 트레저즈.
또 방들은 지식으로 말미암아 각종 귀하고 아름다운 보배로 채우게 되느니라

5 The wise prevail through great power, and those who have knowledge muster their strength.
더 와이즈 프리베일 쓰루 그레이트 파워, 언드 도우즈 후 해브 날러지 머스터 데어 스트렝쓰.
지혜 있는 자는 강하고 지식 있는 자는 힘을 더하나니

6 Surely you need guidance to wage war, and victory is won through many advisers.
슈얼리 유 니드 가이던스 투 웨이지 워어, 언드 빅터어리 이즈 원 쓰루 메니 애드바이저즈.
너는 전략으로 싸우라 승리는 지략이 많음에 있느니라

7 Wisdom is too high for fools; in the assembly at the gate they must not open their mouths.
위즈덤 이즈 투 하이 포어 풀즈 인 디 어셈블리 앳 더 게이트 데이 머스트 낫 오우펀 데어 마운즈.
지혜는 너무 높아서 미련한 자가 미치지 못할 것이므로 그는 성문에서 입을 열지 못하느니라

8 Whoever plots evil will be known as a schemer.
후에버 플랏스 이벌 윌 비 노운 애즈 어 스키머.
악행하기를 꾀하는 자를 일컬어 사악한 자라 하느니라

9 The schemes of folly are sin, and people detest a mocker.
더 스킴즈 어브 팔리 아아 신, 언드 피펄 디테스트 어 마커.
미련한 자의 생각은 죄요 거만한 자는 사람에게 미움을 받느니라

10 If you falter in a time of trouble, how small is your strength!
이프 유 폴터 인 어 타임 어브 트러벌, 하우 스몰 이즈 요어 스트렝쓰!
네가 만일 환난 날에 낙담하면 네 힘이 미약함을 보임이니라

11 Rescue those being led away to death; hold back those staggering toward slaughter.
레스큐 도우즈 비잉 레드 어웨이 투 데쓰 호울드 백 도우즈 스태거링 터워어드 슬로터.
너는 사망으로 끌려가는 자를 건져 주며 살륙을 당하게 된 자를 구원하지 아니하려고 하지 말라

12 If you say, "But we knew nothing about this," does not he who weighs the heart perceive it? Does not he who guards your life know it? Will he not repay everyone according to what they have done?
이프 유 세이, 벗 위 뉴 너씽 어바우트 디스, 더즈 낫 히 후 웨이즈 더 하아트 퍼시브 잇? 더즈 낫 히 후 가아즈 요어 라이프 노우 잇? 윌 히 낫 리페이 에브리원 어코어딩 투 윗 데이 해브 던?
네가 말하기를 나는 그것을 알지 못하였노라 할지라도 마음을 저울질 하시는 이가 어찌 통찰하지 못하시겠으며 네 영혼을 지키시는 이가 어찌 알지 못하시겠느냐 그가 각 사람의 행위대로 보응하시리라

13 Eat honey, my son, for it is good; honey from the comb is sweet to your taste.
잇 허니, 마이 선, 포어 잇 이즈 구드 허니 프럼 더 코움 이즈 스윗 투 요어 테이스트.
내 아들아 꿀을 먹으라 이것이 좋으니라 송이꿀을 먹으라 이것이 네 입에 다니라

14 Know also that wisdom is like honey for you: If you find it, there is a future hope for you, and your hope will not be cut off.
노우 올소우 댓 위즈덤 이즈 라익 허니 포어 유 이프 유 파인드 잇, 데어 이즈 어 퓨처 호웁 포어 유, 언드 요어 호웁 윌 낫 비 컷 오프.
지혜가 네 영혼에게 이와 같은 줄을 알라 이것을 얻으면 정녕히 네 장래가 있겠고 네 소망이 끊어지지 아니하리라

15 Do not lurk like a thief near the house of the righteous, do not plunder their dwelling place;
두 낫 럭 라익 어 씨프 니어 더 하우스 어브 더 라이처스, 두 낫 플런더 데어 웰링 플레이스
악한 자여 의인의 집을 엿보지 말며 그가 쉬는 처소를 헐지 말지니라

16 for though the righteous fall seven times, they rise again, but the wicked stumble when calamity strikes.
포어 도우 더 라이처스 폴 세번 타임즈, 데이 라이즈 어겐, 벗 더 위커드 스텀벌 웬 컬래머티 스트라익스.
대저 의인은 일곱 번 넘어질지라도 다시 일어나려니와 악인은 재앙으로 말미암아 엎드러지느니라

17 Do not gloat when your enemy falls; when they stumble, do not let your heart rejoice,
두 낫 글로우트 웬 요어 에너미 폴즈 웬 데이 스텀벌, 두 낫 렛 요어 하아트 리조이스.

네 원수가 넘어질 때에 즐거워하지 말며 그가 엎드러질 때에 마음에 기뻐하지 말라

18 or the LORD will see and disapprove and turn his wrath away from them.
오어 더 로어드 윌 시 언드 디섭루브 언드 턴 히즈 래쓰 어웨이 프럼 뎀.
여호와께서 이것을 보시고 기뻐하지 아니하사 그의 진노를 그에게서 옮기실까 두려우니라

19 Do not fret because of evildoers or be envious of the wicked,
두 낫 프렛 비카즈 어브 이벌두어즈 오어 비 엔비어스 어브 더 위커드.
너는 행악자들로 말미암아 분을 품지 말며 악인의 형통함을 부러워하지 말라

20 for the evildoer has no future hope, and the lamp of the wicked will be snuffed out.
포어 디 이벌두어 해즈 노우 퓨처 호웊, 언드 더 램프 어브 더 위커드 윌 비 스너프트 아웃.
대저 행악자는 장래가 없겠고 악인의 등불은 꺼지리라

21 Fear the LORD and the king, my son, and do not join with rebellious officials,
피어 더 로어드 언드 더 킹, 마이 선, 언드 두 낫 조인 윋 리벨려스 어피셜즈.
내 아들아 여호와와 왕을 경외하고 반역자와 더불어 사귀지 말라

22 for those two will send sudden destruction on them, and who knows what calamities they can bring?
포어 도우즈 투 윌 센드 서던 디스트럭션 안 뎀, 언드 후 노우즈 웟 컬래머티즈 데이 캔 브링?
대저 그들의 재앙은 속히 임하리니 그 둘의 멸망을 누가 알랴

23 These also are sayings of the wise: To show partiality in judging is not good:
디즈 올소우 아아 세이잉즈 어브 더 와이즈 투 쇼우 파아쉬앨러티 인 저징 이즈 낫 구드
이것도 지혜로운 자들의 말씀이라 재판할 때에 낯을 보아 주는 것이 옳지 못하니라

24 Whoever says to the guilty, "You are innocent," will be cursed by peoples and denounced by nations.
후에버 세즈 투 더 길티, 유 아아 이너선트, 윌 비 커스트 바이 피펄즈 언드 디나운스트 바이 네이션즈.
악인에게 네가 옳다 하는 자는 백성에게 저주를 받을 것이요 국민에게 미움을 받으려니와

25 But it will go well with those who convict the guilty, and rich blessing will come on them.
벗 잇 윌 고우 웰 윋 도우즈 후 컨빅트 더 길티, 언드 리치 블레싱 윌 컴 안 뎀.
오직 그를 견책하는 자는 기쁨을 얻을 것이요 또 좋은 복을 받으리라

26 An honest answer is like a kiss on the lips.
앤 아너스트 앤서 이즈 라익 어 키스 안 더 립스.
적당한 말로 대답함은 입맞춤과 같으니라

27 Put your outdoor work in order and get your fields ready; after that, build your house.
풋 요어 아웃도어 웍 인 오어더 언드 겟 요어 필즈 레디 애프터 댓, 빌드 요어 하우스.
네 일을 밖에서 다스리며 너를 위하여 밭에서 준비하고 그 후에 네 집을 세울지니라

28 Do not testify against your neighbor without cause—would you use your lips to mislead？
두 낫 테스티파이 어겐스트 요어 네이버 위다우트 코즈 워드 유 유스 요어 립스 투 미슬리드?
너는 까닭 없이 네 이웃을 쳐서 증인이 되지 말며 네 입술로 속이지 말지니라

29 Do not say, "I'll do to them as they have done to me; I'll pay them back for what they did."
두 낫 세이, 아일 두 투 뎀 애즈 데이 해브 던 투 미 아일 페이 뎀 백 포어 웟 데이 디드.

너는 그가 내게 행함 같이 나도 그에게 행하여 그가 행한 대로 그 사람에게 갚겠다 말하지 말지니라

30 I went past the field of the sluggard, past the vineyard of someone who has no sense;
아이 웬트 패스트 더 필드 어브 더 슬러거드, 패스트 더 비느여드 어브 서뭔 후 해즈 노우 센스
내가 게으른 자의 밭과 지혜 없는 자의 포도원을 지나며 본즉

31 thorns had come up everywhere, the ground was covered with weeds, and the stone wall was in ruins.
쏜즈 해드 컴 업 에브리웨어, 더 그라운드 와즈 커버드 윋 위즈, 언드 더 스토운 월 와즈 인 루언즈.
가시덤불이 그 전부에 퍼졌으며 그 지면이 거친 풀로 덮였고 돌담이 무너져 있기로

32 I applied my heart to what I observed and learned a lesson from what I saw:
아이 업라이드 마이 하아트 투 윗 아이 어브저브드 언드 런드 어 레선 프럼 윗 아이 소
내가 보고 생각이 깊었고 내가 보고 훈계를 받았노라

33 A little sleep, a little slumber, a little folding of the hands to rest—
어 리털 슬립, 어 리털 슬럼버, 어 리털 포울딩 어브 더 핸즈 투 레스트
네가 좀더 자자, 좀더 졸자, 손을 모으고 좀더 누워 있자 하니

34 and poverty will come on you like a thief and scarcity like an armed man.
언드 파버티 윌 컴 안 유 라익 어 씨프 언드 스케어시티 라익 앤 아아므드 맨.
네 빈궁이 강도 같이 오며 네 곤핍이 군사 같이 이르리라

company [kʌ́mpəni] n. 떼
talk [tɔːk] vi. 말하다
rare [rɛər] a. 드문, 진기한
beautiful [bjúːtəfəl] a. 아름다운
prevail [privéil] vi. 우세하다
muster [mʌ́stər] n. 소집, 검열
war [wɔːr] n. 전쟁, 싸움
victory [víktəri] n. 승리, 전승
falter [fɔ́ːltər] vi. 비틀거리다
hold [hould] vt. 갖고 있다
slaughter [slɔ́ːtər] n. 도살
perceive [pərsíːv] vt. 지각하다
taste [teist] n. 미각
future [fjúːtʃər] n. 미래
hope [houp] n. 희망
cut [kʌt] vt. 베다
thief [θiːf] n. 도둑
enemy [énəmi] n. 적, 원수
partiality [pɑ̀ːrʃiǽləti] n. 편파
denounce [dináuns] vt. 비난하다
rebellious [ribéljəs] a. 반역하는
official [əfíʃəl] a. 공무상의
weed [wiːd] n. 잡초, 해초
observe [əbzə́ːrv] vi. 관찰하다

25장

1 These are more proverbs of Solomon, compiled by the men of Hezekiah king of Judah:
디즈 아아 모어 프라버브즈 어브 살러먼, 컴파일드 바이 더 멘 어브 헤지키어 킹 어브 주더
이것도 솔로몬의 잠언이요 유다 왕 히스기야의 신하들이 편집한 것이니라

2 It is the glory of God to conceal a matter; to search out a matter is the glory of kings.
잇 이즈 더 글로어리 어브 가드 투 컨실 어 매터 투 서치 아웃 어 매터 이즈 더 글로어리 어브 킹즈.
일을 숨기는 것은 하나님의 영화요 일을 살피는 것은 왕의 영화니라

3 As the heavens are high and the earth is deep, so the hearts of kings are unsearchable.
애즈 더 헤번즈 아아 하이 언드 디 어쓰 이즈 딥, 소우 더 하아트스 어브 킹즈 아아 언서처벌.
하늘의 높음과 땅의 깊음 같이 왕의 마음은 헤아릴 수 없느니라

4 Remove the dross from the silver, and a silversmith can produce a vessel;
리무브 더 드로스 프럼 더 실버, 언드 어 실버스미쓰 캔 프러두스 어 베설
은에서 찌꺼기를 제하라 그리하면 장색의 쓸 만한 그릇이 나올 것이요

5 remove wicked officials from the king's presence, and his throne will be established through

righteousness.
리무브 위커드 어피셜즈 프럼 더 킹즈 프레전스, 언드 히즈 쓰로운 윌 비 이스태블리쉬 트쓰루 라이처스너스.
왕 앞에서 악한 자를 제하라 그리하면 그의 왕위가 의로 말미암아 견고히 서리라

6 Do not exalt yourself in the king's presence, and do not claim a place among his great men;
두 낫 이그졸트 요어셀프 인 더 킹즈 프레전스, 언드 두 낫 클레임 어 플레이스 어멍 히즈 그레이트 멘
왕 앞에서 스스로 높은 체하지 말며 대인들의 자리에 서지 말라

7 it is better for him to say to you, "Come up here," than for him to humiliate you before his nobles. What you have seen with your eyes
잇 이즈 베터 포어 힘 투 세이 투 유, 컴 업 히어, 던 포어 힘 투 휴밀리에잇 유 비포어 히즈 노우벌즈. 웟 유 해브 신 윋 요어 아이즈
이는 사람이 네게 이리로 올라오라고 말하는 것이 네 눈에 보이는 귀인 앞에서 저리로 내려가라고 말하는 것보다 나음이니라

8 do not bring hastily to court, for what will you do in the end if your neighbor puts you to shame?
두 낫 브링 헤이스털리 투 코어트, 포어 웟 윌 유 두 인 디 엔드 이프 요어 네이버 풋스 유 투 셰임?
너는 서둘러 나가서 다투지 말라 마침내 네가 이웃에게서 욕을 보게 될 때에 네가 어찌할 줄을 알지 못할까 두려우니라

9 If you take your neighbor to court, do not betray another's confidence,
이프 유 테익 요어 네이버 투 코어트, 두 낫 빗레이 어너더즈 칸퍼덴스.
너는 이웃과 다투거든 변론만 하고 남의 은밀한 일은 누설하지 말라

10 or the one who hears it may shame you and the charge against you will stand.
오어 더 원 후 히어즈 잇 메이 셰임 유 언드 더 차아지 어겐스트 유 윌 스탠드.
듣는 자가 너를 꾸짖을 터이요 또 네게 대한 악평이 네게서 떠나지 아니할까 두려우니라

11 Like apples of gold in settings of silver is a ruling rightly given.
라익 애펄즈 어브 고울드 인 세팅즈 어브 실버 이즈 어 룰링 라잇리 기번.
경우에 합당한 말은 아로새긴 은 쟁반에 금 사과니라

12 Like an earring of gold or an ornament of fine gold is the rebuke of a wise judge to a listening ear.
라익 앤 이어링 어브 고울드 오어 앤 오어너먼트 어브 파인 고울드 이즈 더 리뷱 어브 어 와이즈 저지 투 어 리서닝 이어.
슬기로운 자의 책망은 청종하는 귀에 금 고리와 정금 장식이니라

13 Like a snowcooled drink at harvest time is a trustworthy messenger to the one who sends him; he refreshes the spirit of his master.
라익 어 스노우쿨드 드링크 앳 하아버스트 타임 이즈 어 트러스트워디 메선저 투 디 원 후 센즈 힘 히 리프레쉬즈 더 스피럿 어브 히즈 매스터.
충성된 사자는 그를 보낸 이에게 마치 추수하는 날에 얼음 냉수 같아서 능히 그 주인의 마음을 시원하게 하느니라

14 Like clouds and wind without rain is one who boasts of gifts never given.
라익 클라우즈 언드 윈드 위다우트 레인 이즈 원 후 보우스트스 어브 기프트스 네버 기번.
선물한다고 거짓 자랑하는 자는 비 없는 구름과 바람 같으니라

15 Through patience a ruler can be persuaded, and a gentle tongue can break a bone.

쓰루 페이션스 어 룰러 캔 비 퍼쉐더드, 언드 어 젠털 텅 캔 브레익 어 보운.

오래 참으면 관원도 설득할 수 있나니 부드러운 혀는 뼈를 꺾느니라

16 If you find honey, eat just enough—too much of it, and you will vomit.

이프 유 파인드 허니, 잇 저스트 이너프 투 머치 어브 잇, 언드 유 윌 바멋.

너는 꿀을 보거든 족하리만큼 먹으라 과식함으로 토할까 두려우니라

17 Seldom set foot in your neighbor's house—too much of you, and they will hate you.

셀덤 셋 풋 인 요어 네이버즈 하우스 투 머치 어브 유, 언드 데이 윌 헤이트 유.

너는 이웃집에 자주 다니지 말라 그가 너를 싫어하며 미워할까 두려우니라

18 Like a club or a sword or a sharp arrow is one who gives false testimony against a neighbor.

라익 어 클러브 오어 어 소어드 오어 어 샤아프 애어로우 이즈 원 후 기브즈 폴스 테스티모우니 어겐스트 어 네이버.

자기의 이웃을 쳐서 거짓 증거하는 사람은 방망이요 칼이요 뾰족한 화살이니라

19 Like a broken tooth or a lame foot is reliance on the unfaithful in a time of trouble.

라익 어 브로우컨 투쓰 오어 어 레임 풋 이즈 릴라이언스 안 디 언페이쓰펄 인 어 타임 어브 트러벌.

환난 날에 진실하지 못한 자를 의뢰하는 것은 부러진 이와 위골된 발 같으니라

20 Like one who takes away a garment on a cold day, or like vinegar poured on a wound, is one who sings songs to a heavy heart.

라익 원 후 테익스 어웨이 어 가아먼트 안 어 코울드 데이, 오어 라익 비너거 포어드 안 어 와운드, 이즈 원 후 싱즈 송즈 투 어 헤비 하아트.

마음이 상한 자에게 노래하는 것은 추운 날에 옷을 벗음 같고 소다 위에 식초를 부음 같으니라

21 If your enemy is hungry, give him food to eat; if he is thirsty, give him water to drink.

이프 요어 에너미 이즈 헝그리, 기브 힘 푸드 투 잇 이프 히 이즈 써스티, 기브 힘 워터 투 드링크.

네 원수가 배고파하거든 음식을 먹이고 목말라하거든 물을 마시게 하라

22 In doing this, you will heap burning coals on his head, and the LORD will reward you.

인 두잉 디스, 유 윌 힙 버닝 코울즈 안 히즈 헤드, 언드 더 로어드 윌 리워어드 유.

그리하는 것은 핀 숯을 그의 머리에 놓는 것과 일반이요 여호와께서 네게 갚아 주시리라

23 Like a north wind that brings unexpected rain is a sly tongue—which provokes a horrified look.

라익 어 노어쓰 윈드 댓 브링즈 어닉스펙티드 레인 이즈 어 슬라이 텅 위치 프러보욱스 어 호어러파이드 룩.

북풍이 비를 일으킴 같이 참소하는 혀는 사람의 얼굴에 분을 일으키느니라

24 Better to live on a corner of the roof than share a house with a quarrelsome wife.

베터 투 리브 안 어 코어너 어브 더 루프 던 셰어 어 하우스 윋 어 쿼럴섬 와이프.

다투는 여인과 함께 큰 집에서 사는 것보다 움막에서 혼자 사는 것이 나으니라

25 Like cold water to a weary soul is good news from a distant land.

라익 코울드 워터 투 어 위리 소울 이즈 구드 뉴즈 프럼 어 디스턴트 랜드.

먼 땅에서 오는 좋은 기별은 목마른 사람에게 냉수와 같으니라

26 Like a muddied spring or a polluted well are the righteous who give way to the wicked.

라익 어 머디드 스프링 오어 어 펄루터드 웰 아아 더 라이처스 후 기브 웨이 투 더 위커드.

의인이 악인 앞에 굴복하는 것은 우물이 흐려짐과 샘이 더러워짐과 같으니라

27 It is not good to eat too much honey, nor is it honorable to search out matters that are too deep.

잇 이즈 낫 구드 투 잇 투 머치 허니, 노어 이즈 잇 아너러벌 투 서치 아웃 매터즈 댓 아아 투 딥.
꿀을 많이 먹는 것이 좋지 못하고 자기의 영예를 구하는 것이 헛되니라

28 Like a city whose walls are broken through is a person who lacks self-control.
라익 어 시티 후즈 월즈 아아 브로우 컨쓰루 이즈 어 퍼선 후 랙스 셀프컨트로울.
자기의 마음을 제어하지 아니하는 자는 성읍이 무너지고 성벽이 없는 것과 같으니라

compile [kəmpáil] vt. 편집하다
matter [mǽtər] n. 물질
search [səːrtʃ] vt. 찾다, 뒤지다
glory [glɔ́ːri] n. 영광, 명예
remove [rimúːv] vt. …을 옮기다
dross [drɔːs] n. 뜬 찌끼, 불순물
vessel [vésəl] n. 용기, 그릇
charge [tʃɑːrdʒ] vt. 충전하다
among [əmʌ́ŋ] prep. …의 사이에
humiliate [hjuːmílièit] vt. 욕보이다
noble [nóubəl] a. 귀족의
hastily [héistili] ad. 바삐, 급히
ruling [rúːliŋ] a. 지배하는
rightly [ráitli] ad. 올바르게
earring [íəriŋ] n. 귀고리
ornament [ɔ́ːrnəmənt] n. 꾸밈
boast [boust] vi. 자랑하다
persuade [pəːrswéid] vt. 설득하다
arrow [ǽrou] n. 화살
testimony [téstəmòuni] n. 증언
distant [dístənt] a. 먼, 떨어진
pollute [pəlúːt] vt. 더럽히다
honorable [ɑ́nərəbəl] a. 명예로운
provoke [prəvóuk] vt. 일으키다

26장 1 Like snow in summer or rain in harvest, honor is not fitting for a fool.
라익 스노우 인 서머 오어 레인 인 하아버스트, 아너 이즈 낫 피팅 포어 어 풀.
미련한 자에게는 영예가 적당하지 아니하니 마치 여름에 눈 오는 것과 추수 때에 비 오는 것 같으니라

2 Like a fluttering sparrow or a darting swallow, an undeserved curse does not come to rest.
라익 어 플러터링 스페어로우 오어 어 다아팅 스왈로우, 앤 언디저브드 커스 더즈 낫 컴 투 레스트.
까닭 없는 저주는 참새가 떠도는 것과 제비가 날아가는 것 같이 이루어지지 아니하느니라

3 A whip for the horse, a bridle for the donkey, and a rod for the backs of fools!
어 윕 포어 더 호어스, 어 브라이덜 포어 더 당키, 언드 어 라드 포어 더 백스 어브 풀즈!
말에게는 채찍이요 나귀에게는 재갈이요 미련한 자의 등에는 막대기니라

4 Do not answer a fool according to his folly, or you yourself will be just like him.
두 낫 앤서 어 풀 어코어딩 투 히즈 팔리, 오어 유 요어셀프 윌 비 저스트 라익 힘.
미련한 자의 어리석은 것을 따라 대답하지 말라 두렵건대 너도 그와 같을까 하노라

5 Answer a fool according to his folly, or he will be wise in his own eyes.
앤서 어 풀 어코어딩 투 히즈 팔리, 오어 히 윌 비 와이즈 인 히즈 오운 아이즈.
미련한 자에게는 그의 어리석음을 따라 대답하라 두렵건대 그가 스스로 지혜롭게 여길까 하노라

6 Sending a message by the hands of a fool is like cutting off one's feet or drinking poison.
센딩 어 메서지 바이 더 핸즈 어브 어 풀 이즈 라익 커팅 오프 원즈 핏 오어 드링킹 포이전.
미련한 자 편에 기별하는 것은 자기의 발을 베어 버림과 해를 받음과 같으니라

7 Like the useless legs of one who is lame is a proverb in the mouth of a fool.
라익 더 유슬러스 레그즈 어브 원 후 이즈 레임 이즈 어 프라버브 인 더 마우쓰 어브 어 풀.
저는 자의 다리는 힘 없이 달렸나니 미련한 자의 입의 잠언도 그러하니라

8 Like tying a stone in a sling is the giving of honor to a fool.
라익 타이잉 어 스토운 인 어 슬링 이즈 더 기빙 어브 아너 투 어 풀.
미련한 자에게 영예를 주는 것은 돌을 물매에 매는 것과 같으니라

9 Like a thornbush in a drunkard's hand is a proverb in the mouth of a fool.

라익 어 쏜부쉬 인 어 드렁커즈 핸드 이즈 어 프라버브 인 더 마우쓰 어브 어 풀.
미련한 자의 입의 잠언은 술 취한 자가 손에 든 가시나무 같으니라

10 Like an archer who wounds at random is one who hires a fool or any passer-by.
라익 앤 아아처 후 원즈 앳 랜덤 이즈 원 후 하여즈 어 풀 오어 에니 패서바이.
장인이 온갖 것을 만들지라도 미련한 자를 고용하는 것은 지나가는 행인을 고용함과 같으니라

11 As a dog returns to its vomit, so fools repeat their folly.
애즈 어 도그 리턴즈 투 잇스 바멋, 소우 풀즈 리핏 데어 팔리.
개가 그 토한 것을 도로 먹는 것 같이 미련한 자는 그 미련한 것을 거듭 행하느니라

12 Do you see a person wise in their own eyes? There is more hope for a fool than for them.
두 유 시 어 퍼선 와이즈 인 데어 오운 아이즈? 데어 이즈 모어 호웁 포어 어 풀 던 포어 뎀.
네가 스스로 지혜롭게 여기는 자를 보느냐 그보다 미련한 자에게 오히려 희망이 있느니라

13 A sluggard says, "There's a lion in the road, a fierce lion roaming the streets!"
어 슬러거드 세즈, 데어즈 어 라이언 인 더 로우드, 어 피어스 라이언 로우밍 더 스트릿스!
게으른 자는 길에 사자가 있다 거리에 사자가 있다 하느니라

14 As a door turns on its hinges, so a sluggard turns on his bed.
애즈 어 도어 턴즈 안 잇스 힌지즈, 소우 어 슬러거드 턴즈 안 히즈 베드.
문짝이 돌쩌귀를 따라서 도는 것 같이 게으른 자는 침상에서 도느니라

15 A sluggard buries his hand in the dish; he is too lazy to bring it back to his mouth.
어 슬러거드 베어리즈 히즈 핸드 인 더 디쉬 히 이즈 투 레이지 투 브링 잇 백 투 히즈 마우쓰.
게으른 자는 그 손을 그릇에 넣고도 입으로 올리기를 괴로워하느니라

16 A sluggard is wiser in his own eyes than seven people who answer discreetly.
어 슬러거드 이즈 와이저 인 히즈 오운 아이즈 던 세번 피펄 후 앤서 디스크리틀리.
게으른 자는 사리에 맞게 대답하는 사람 일곱보다 자기를 지혜롭게 여기느니라

17 Like one who grabs a stray dog by the ears is someone who rushes into a quarrel not their own.
라익 원 후 그래브즈 어 스트레이 도그 바이 디 이어즈 이즈 서원 후 러셔즈 인투 어 쿼럴 낫 데어 오운.
길로 지나가다가 자기와 상관 없는 다툼을 간섭하는 자는 개의 귀를 잡는 자와 같으니라

18 Like a maniac shooting flaming arrows of death
라익 어 메이니 액슈팅 플레이밍 애어로우즈 어브 데쓰
횃불을 던지며 화살을 쏘아서 사람을 죽이는 미친 사람이 있나니

19 is one who deceives their neighbor and says, "I was only joking!"
이즈 원 후 디시브즈 데어 네이버 언드 세즈, 아이 와즈 오운리 조우킹!
자기의 이웃을 속이고 말하기를 내가 희롱하였노라 하는 자도 그러하니라

20 Without wood a fire goes out; without a gossip a quarrel dies down.
위다우트 워드 어 파여 고우즈 아웃 위다우트 어 가섭 어 쿼럴 다이즈 다운.
나무가 다하면 불이 꺼지고 말쟁이가 없어지면 다툼이 쉬느니라

21 As charcoal to embers and as wood to fire, so is a quarrelsome person for kindling strife.
애즈 차아코울 투 엠버즈 언드 애즈 워드 투 파여, 소우 이즈 어 쿼럴섬 퍼선 포어 킨들링 스트라이프.
숯불 위에 숯을 더하는 것과 타는 불에 나무를 더하는 것 같이 다툼을 좋아하는 자는 시비를 일으키느니라

22 The words of a gossip are like choice morsels; they go down to the inmost parts.
더 워즈 어브 어 가섭 아아 라익 초이스 모어설즈 데이 고우 다운 투 디 인모우스트 파아트스.
남의 말 하기를 좋아하는 자의 말은 별식과 같아서 뱃속 깊은 데로 내려가느니라

23 Like a coating of silver dross on earthenware are fervent lips with an evil heart.
라익 어 코우팅 어브 실버 드로스 안 어써웨 아아 퍼번트 립스 윋 앤 이벌 하아트.
온유한 입술에 악한 마음은 낮은 은을 입힌 토기니라

24 Enemies disguise themselves with their lips, but in their hearts they harbor deceit.
에너미즈 디스가이즈 뎀셀브즈 윋 데어 립스, 벗 인 데어 하아트스 데이 하아버 디싯.
원수는 입술로는 꾸미고 속으로는 속임을 품나니

25 Though their speech is charming, do not believe them, for seven abominations fill their hearts.
도우 데어 스피치 이즈 차아밍, 두 낫 빌리브 뎀, 포어 세번 어바머네이션즈 필 데어 하아트스.
그 말이 좋을지라도 믿지 말 것은 그 마음에 일곱 가지 가증한 것이 있음이니라

26 Their malice may be concealed by deception, but their wickedness will be exposed in the assembly.
데어 맬러스 메이 비 컨실드 바이 디셉션, 벗 데어 위커드너스 윌 비 익스포우즈드 인 디 어셈블리.
속임으로 그 미움을 감출지라도 그의 악이 회중 앞에 드러나리라

27 Whoever digs a pit will fall into it; if someone rolls a stone, it will roll back on them.
후에버 디그즈 어 핏 윌 폴 인투 잇 이프 서뭔 로울즈 어 스토운, 잇 윌 로울 백 안 뎀.
함정을 파는 자는 그것에 빠질 것이요 돌을 굴리는 자는 도리어 그것에 치이리라

28 A lying tongue hates those it hurts, and a flattering mouth works ruin.
어 라이잉 텅 헤잇스 도우즈 잇 허트스, 언드 어 플래터링 마우쓰 웍스 루언.
거짓말하는 자는 자기가 해한 자를 미워하고 아첨하는 입은 패망을 일으키느니라

summer [sʌ́mər] n. 여름	lame [leim] a. 절름발이의	shoot [ʃuːt] vt. 쏘다, 발사하다
flutter [flʌ́tər] vi. 퍼덕거리다	sling [sliŋ] n. 투석기, 새총	flaming [fléimiŋ] a. 타오르는
sparrow [spǽrou] n. 참새	archer [άːrtʃər] n. 사수, 궁술가	charcoal [tʃάːrkòul] n. 숯, 목탄
curse [kəːrs] vt. 저주하다	wound [wuːnd] n. 부상, 상처	ember [émbər] n. 타다 남은 것
whip [hwip] vt. 채찍질하다	random [rǽndəm] a. 임의의	disguise [disgáiz] n. 변장, 가장
bridle [bráidl] n. 굴레	hire [haiər] vt. 고용하다	malice [mǽlis] n. 악의, 해할 마음
poison [pɔ́izən] n. 독, 독물	grab [græb] vt. 움켜잡다	harbor [hάːrbər] n. 항구
useless [júːslis] a. 쓸모없는	maniac [méiniæ̀k] a. 미친, 발광한	roll [roul] vi. 구르다

27장 1 Do not boast about tomorrow, for you do not know what a day may bring.
두 낫 보우스트 어바우트 터마아로우, 포어 유 두 낫 노우 웟 어 데이 메이 브링.
너는 내일 일을 자랑하지 말라 하루 동안에 무슨 일이 일어날는지 네가 알 수 없음이니라

2 Let someone else praise you, and not your own mouth; an outsider, and not your own lips.
렛 서뭔 엘스 프레이즈 유, 언드 낫 요어 오운 마우쓰 앤 아웃사이더, 언드 낫 요어 오운 립스.
타인이 너를 칭찬하게 하고 네 입으로는 하지 말며 외인이 너를 칭찬하게 하고 네 입술로는 하지 말지니라

3 Stone is heavy and sand a burden, but a fool's provocation is heavier than both.
스토운 이즈 헤비 언드 샌드 어 버던, 벗 어 풀즈 프라버케이션 이즈 헤비어 던 보우쓰.

돌은 무겁고 모래도 가볍지 아니하거니와 미련한 자의 분노는 이 둘보다 무거우니라

4 Anger is cruel and fury overwhelming, but who can stand before jealousy?
앵거 이즈 크루얼 언드 퓨리 오우버웰밍, 벗 후 캔 스탠드 비포어 젤러시?
분은 잔인하고 노는 창수 같거니와 투기 앞에야 누가 서리요

5 Better is open rebuke than hidden love.
베터 이즈 오우펀 리뷰크 던 히던 러브.
면책은 숨은 사랑보다 나으니라

6 Wounds from a friend can be trusted, but an enemy multiplies kisses.
원즈 프럼 어 프렌드 캔 비 트러스티드, 벗 앤 에너미 멀터플라이즈 키서즈.
친구의 아픈 책망은 충직으로 말미암는 것이나 원수의 잦은 입맞춤은 거짓에서 난 것이니라

7 One who is full loathes honey from the comb, but to the hungry even what is bitter tastes sweet.
원 후 이즈 풀 로웉즈 허니 프럼 더 코움, 벗 투 더 헝그리 이빈 웟 이즈 비터 테이스트스 스윗.
배부른 자는 꿀이라도 싫어하고 주린 자에게는 쓴 것이라도 다니라

8 Like a bird that flees its nest is anyone who flees from home.
라익 어 버드 댓 플리즈 잇스 네스트 이즈 에니원 후 플리즈 프럼 호움.
고향을 떠나 유리하는 사람은 보금자리를 떠나 떠도는 새와 같으니라

9 Perfume and incense bring joy to the heart, and the pleasantness of a friend springs from their heartfelt advice.
퍼퓸 언드 인센스 브링 조이 투 더 하아트, 언드 더 플레전트너스 어브 어 프렌드 스프링즈 프럼 데어 하아트펠트 애드바이스.
기름과 향이 사람의 마음을 즐겁게 하나니 친구의 충성된 권고가 이와 같이 아름다우니라

10 Do not forsake your friend or a friend of your family, and do not go to your relative's house when disaster strikes you—better a neighbor nearby than a relative far away.
두 낫 포어세익 요어 프렌드 오어 어 프렌드 어브 요어 패멀리, 언드 두 낫 고우 투 요어 렐러티브즈 하우스 웬 디재스터 스트라익스 유 베터 어 네이버 니어바이 던 어 렐러티브 파아 어웨이.
네 친구와 네 아비의 친구를 버리지 말며 네 환난 날에 형제의 집에 들어가지 말지어다 가까운 이웃이 먼 형제보다 나으니라

11 Be wise, my son, and bring joy to my heart; then I can answer anyone who treats me with contempt.
비 와이즈, 마이 선, 언드 브링 조이 투 마이 하아트 덴 아이 캔 앤서 에니원 후 트릿스 미 윋 컨템프트.
내 아들아 지혜를 얻고 내 마음을 기쁘게 하라 그리하면 나를 비방하는 자에게 내가 대답할 수 있으리라

12 The prudent see danger and take refuge, but the simple keep going and pay the penalty.
더 프루던트 시 데인저 언드 테익 레퓨지, 벗 더 심펄 킵 고우잉 언드 페이 더 페널티.
슬기로운 자는 재앙을 보면 숨어 피하여도 어리석은 자들은 나가다가 해를 받느니라

13 Take the garment of one who puts up security for a stranger; hold it in pledge if it is done for an outsider.
테익 더 가아먼트 어브 원 후 풋스 업 시큐러티 포어 어 스트레인저 호울드 잇 인 플레지 이프 잇 이즈 던 포어 앤 아웃사이더.

타인을 위하여 보증 선 자의 옷을 취하라 외인들을 위하여 보증 선 자는 그의 몸을 볼모 잡을지니라

14 If anyone loudly blesses their neighbor early in the morning, it will be taken as a curse.
이프 에니원 라우들리 블레시즈 데어 네이버 얼리 인 더 모어닝, 잇 윌 비 테이컨 애즈 어 커스.
이른 아침에 큰 소리로 자기 이웃을 축복하면 도리어 저주 같이 여기게 되리라

15 A quarrelsome wife is like the dripping of a leaky roof in a rainstorm;
어 쿼럴섬 와이프 이즈 라익 더 드리핑 어브 어 리키 루프 인 어 레인스톰
다투는 여자는 비 오는 날에 이어 떨어지는 물방울이라

16 restraining her is like restraining the wind or grasping oil with the hand.
리스트레이닝 허 이즈 라익 리스트레이닝 더 윈드 오어 그래스핑 오일 윋 더 핸드.
그를 제어하기가 바람을 제어하는 것 같고 오른손으로 기름을 움키는 것 같으니라

17 As iron sharpens iron, so one person sharpens another.
애즈 아이어느 샤아펀즈 아이어느, 소우 원 퍼선 샤아펀즈 어너더.
철이 철을 날카롭게 하는 것 같이 사람이 그의 친구의 얼굴을 빛나게 하느니라

18 The one who guards a fig tree will eat its fruit, and whoever protects their master will be honored.
디 원 후 가아즈 어 피그 트리 윌 잇 잇스 프룻, 언드 후에버 프러텍트스 데어 매스터 윌 비 아너드.
무화과나무를 지키는 자는 그 과실을 먹고 자기 주인에게 시중드는 자는 영화를 얻느니라

19 As water reflects the face, so one's life reflects the heart.
애즈 워터 리플렉트스 더 페이스, 소우 원즈 라이프 리플렉트스 더 하아트.
물에 비치면 얼굴이 서로 같은 것 같이 사람의 마음도 서로 비치느니라

20 Death and Destruction are never satisfied, and neither are human eyes.
데쓰 언드 디스트럭션 아아 네버 새터스파이드, 언드 나이더 아아 휴먼 아이즈.
스올과 아바돈은 만족함이 없고 사람의 눈도 만족함이 없느니라

21 The crucible for silver and the furnace for gold, but people are tested by their praise.
더 크루서벌 포어 실버 언드 더 퍼너스 포어 고울드, 벗 피펄 아아 테스티드 바이 데어 프레이즈.
도가니로 은을, 풀무로 금을, 칭찬으로 사람을 단련하느니라

22 Though you grind a fool in a mortar, grinding them like grain with a pestle, you will not remove their folly from them.
도우 유 그라인드 어 풀 인 어 모어터, 그라인딩 뎀 라익 그레인 윋 어 페설, 유 윌 낫 리무브 데어 팔리 프럼 뎀.
미련한 자를 곡물과 함께 절구에 넣고 공이로 찧을지라도 그의 미련은 벗겨지지 아니하느니라

23 Be sure you know the condition of your flocks, give careful attention to your herds;
비 슈어 유 노우 더 컨디션 어브 요어 플락스, 기브 케어펄 어텐션 투 요어 허즈
네 양 떼의 형편을 부지런히 살피며 네 소 떼에게 마음을 두라

24 for riches do not endure forever, and a crown is not secure for all generations.
포어 리처즈 두 낫 엔듀 퍼레버, 언드 어 크라운 이즈 낫 시큐 포어 올 제너레이션즈.
대저 재물은 영원히 있지 못하나니 면류관이 어찌 대대에 있으랴

25 When the hay is removed and new growth appears and the grass from the hills is gathered in,
웬 더 헤이 이즈 리무브드 언드 누 그로우쓰 어피어즈 언드 더 그래스 프럼 더 힐즈 이즈 개더드 인.
풀을 벤 후에는 새로 움이 돋나니 산에서 꼴을 거둘 것이니라

26 the lambs will provide you with clothing, and the goats with the price of a field.
더 램즈 윌 프러바이드 유 윋 클로우딩, 언드 더 고웃스 윋 더 프라이스 어브 어 필드.
어린 양의 털은 네 옷이 되며 염소는 밭을 사는 값이 되며

27 You will have plenty of goats' milk to feed your family and to nourish your female servants.
유 윌 해브 플렌티 어브 고웃스 밀크 투 피드 요어 패멀리 언드 투 너리쉬 요어 피메일 서번트스.
염소의 젖은 넉넉하여 너와 네 집의 음식이 되며 네 여종의 먹을 것이 되느니라

sand [sænd] n. 모래	treat [triːt] vt. 다루다	grind [graind] vt. 갈다
burden [bəːrdn] n. 무거운 짐, 짐	garment [gɑ́ːrmənt] n. 의복	grain [grein] n. 낟알, 곡물
hidden [hídn] a. 숨은	leaky [líːki] a. 새기 쉬운	pestle [péstl] n. 빻는 기계, 공이
loathe [louð] vt. 몹시 싫어하다	restrain [ristréin] vt. 제지하다	hill [hil] n. 언덕
flee [fliː] vi. 달아나다	grasp [græsp] vt. 붙잡다	price [prais] n. 가격, 대가
nest [nest] n.보금자리, 둥우리	iron [áiərn] n. 철	plenty [plénti] n. 많음, 가득
anyone [éniwʌ̀n] pron. 누구도	reflect [riflékt] vt. 반사하다	goat [gout] n. 염소
incense [ínsens] n. 향, 향냄새	face [feis] n. 얼굴	secure [sikjúər] a. 안전한

28장 1 The wicked flee though no one pursues, but the righteous are as bold as a lion.
더 위커드 플리 도우 노우 원 퍼수즈, 벗 더 라이처스 아아 애즈 보울드 애즈 어 라이언.
악인은 쫓아오는 자가 없어도 도망하나 의인은 사자 같이 담대하니라

2 When a country is rebellious, it has many rulers, but a ruler with discernment and knowledge maintains order.
웬 어 컨트리 이즈 리벨려스, 잇 해즈 메니 룰러즈, 벗 어 룰러 윋 디선먼트 언드 날러지 메인테인즈 오어더.
나라는 죄가 있으면 주관자가 많아져도 명철과 지식 있는 사람으로 말미암아 장구하게 되느니라

3 A ruler who oppresses the poor is like a driving rain that leaves no crops.
어 룰러 후 업레시즈 더 푸어 이즈 라익 어 드라이빙 레인 댓 리브즈 노우 크랍스.
가난한 자를 학대하는 가난한 자는 곡식을 남기지 아니하는 폭우 같으니라

4 Those who forsake instruction praise the wicked, but those who heed it resist them.
도우즈 후 포어세익 인스트럭션 프레이즈 더 위커드, 벗 도우즈 후 히드 잇 리지스트 뎀.
율법을 버린 자는 악인을 칭찬하나 율법을 지키는 자는 악인을 대적하느니라

5 Evildoers do not understand what is right, but those who seek the LORD understand it fully.
이벌두어즈 두 낫 언더스탠드 웟 이즈 라이트, 벗 도우즈 후 식 더 로어드 언더스탠드 잇 풀리.
악인은 정의를 깨닫지 못하나 여호와를 찾는 자는 모든 것을 깨닫느니라

6 Better the poor whose walk is blameless than the rich whose ways are perverse.
베터 더 푸어 후즈 웍 이즈 블레임러스 던 더 리치 후즈 웨이즈 아아 퍼버스.
가난하여도 성실하게 행하는 자는 부유하면서 굽게 행하는 자보다 나으니라

7 A discerning son heeds instruction, but a companion of gluttons disgraces his father.
어 디서닝 선 히즈 인스트럭션, 벗 어 컴패년 어브 글러턴즈 디스그레이시즈 히즈 파더.
율법을 지키는 자는 지혜로운 아들이요 음식을 탐하는 자와 사귀는 자는 아비를 욕되게 하는 자니라

8 Whoever increases wealth by talking interest or profit from the poor amasses it for another, who will be kind to the poor.

후에버 인크리시즈 웰쓰 바이 토킹 인터어레스트 오어 프라펏 프럼 더 푸어 어매시즈 잇 포어 어너더, 후 윌 비 카인드 투 더 푸어.

중한 변리로 자기 재산을 늘이는 것은 가난한 사람을 불쌍히 여기는 자를 위해 그 재산을 저축하는 것이니라

9 If anyone turns a deaf ear to my instruction, even their prayers are detestable.

이프 에니원 턴즈 어 데프 이어 투 마이 인스트럭션, 이빈 데어 프레어즈 아아 디테스터벌.

사람이 귀를 돌려 율법을 듣지 아니하면 그의 기도도 가증하니라

10 Whoever leads the upright along an evil path will fall into their own trap, but the blameless will receive a good inheritance.

후에버 리즈 디 업라이트 얼롱 앤 이벌 패쓰 윌 폴 인투 데어 오운 트랩, 벗 더 블레임러스 윌 러시브 어 구드 인헤러턴스.

정직한 자를 악한 길로 유인하는 자는 스스로 자기 함정에 빠져도 성실한 자는 복을 받느니라

11.The rich are wise in their own eyes; one who is poor and discerning sees how deluded they are.

더 리치 아아 와이즈 인 데어 오운 아이즈 원 후 이즈 푸어 언드 디서닝 시즈 하우 딜루디드 데이 아아.

부자는 자기를 지혜롭게 여기나 가난해도 명철한 자는 자기를 살펴 아느니라

12 When the righteous triumph, there is great elation; but when the wicked rise to power, people go into hiding.

웬 더 라이처스 트라이엄프, 데어 이즈 그레이트 일레이션 벗 웬 더 위커드 라이즈 투 파워, 피펄 고우 인투 하이딩.

의인이 득의하면 큰 영화가 있고 악인이 일어나면 사람이 숨느니라

13 Whoever conceals their sins does not prosper, but the one who confesses and renounces them finds mercy.

후에버 컨실즈 데어 신즈 더즈 낫 프라스퍼, 벗 더 원 후 컨페시즈 언드 리나운시즈 뎀 파인즈 머시.

자기의 죄를 숨기는 자는 형통하지 못하나 죄를 자복하고 버리는 자는 불쌍히 여김을 받으리라

14 Blessed is the one who always trembles before God, but whoever hardens their heart falls into trouble.

블레스트 이즈 더 원 후 올웨이즈 트렘벌즈 비포어 가드, 벗 후에버 하아던즈 데어 하아트 폴즈 인투 트러벌.

항상 경외하는 자는 복되거니와 마음을 완악하게 하는 자는 재앙에 빠지리라

15.Like a roaring lion or a charging bear is a wicked ruler over a helpless people.

라익 어 로링 라이언 오어 어 차아징 베어 이즈 어 위커드 룰러 오우버 어 헬플러스 피펄.

가난한 백성을 압제하는 악한 관원은 부르짖는 사자와 주린 곰 같으니라

16.A tyrannical ruler practices extortion, but one who hates ill-gotten gain will enjoy a long reign.

어 터래니컬 룰러 프랙티시즈 엑스토어션, 벗 원 후 헤잇스 일가턴 게인 윌 엔조이 어 롱 레인.

무지한 치리자는 포학을 크게 행하거니와 탐욕을 미워하는 자는 장수하리라

17.Anyone tormented by the guilt of murder will seek refuge in the grave; let no one hold them back.

에니원 토어멘티드 바이 더 길트 어브 머더 윌 식 레퓨지 인 더 그레이브 렛 노우 원 호울드 뎀 백.

사람의 피를 흘린 자는 함정으로 달려갈 것이니 그를 막지 말지니라

18 The one whose walk is blameless is kept safe, but the one whose ways are perverse will fall into the pit.

더 원 후즈 웍 이즈 블레임러스 이즈 켑트 세이프, 벗 더 원 후즈 웨이즈 아아 퍼버스 윌 폴 인투 더 핏.

성실하게 행하는 자는 구원을 받을 것이나 굽은 길로 행하는 자는 곧 넘어지리라

19 Those who work their land will have abundant food, but those who chase fantasies will have their fill of poverty.
도우즈 후 웍 데어 랜드 윌 해브 어번던트 푸드, 벗 도우즈 후 체이스 팬터시즈 윌 해브 데어 필 어브 파버티.
자기의 토지를 경작하는 자는 먹을 것이 많으려니와 방탕을 따르는 자는 궁핍함이 많으리라

20 A faithful person will be richly blessed, but one eager to get rich will not go unpunished.
어 페이쓰펄 퍼선 윌 비 리츨리 블레스트, 벗 원 이거 투 겟 리치 윌 낫 고우 언퍼니쉬트.
충성된 자는 복이 많아도 속히 부하고자 하는 자는 형벌을 면하지 못하리라

21 To show partiality is not good—yet a person will do wrong for a piece of bread.
투 쇼우 파아쉬앨러티 이즈 낫 구드 옛 어 퍼선 윌 두 롱 포어 어 피스 어브 브레드.
사람의 낯을 보아 주는 것이 좋지 못하고 한 조각 떡으로 말미암아 사람이 범법하는 것도 그러하니라

22 The stingy are eager to get rich and are unaware that poverty awaits them.
더 스틴지 아아 이거 투 겟 리치 언드 아아 어너웨어 댓 파버티 어웨잇스 뎀.
악한 눈이 있는 자는 재물을 얻기에만 급하고 빈궁이 자기에게로 임할 줄은 알지 못하느니라

23 Whoever rebukes a person will in the end gain favor rather than one who has a flattering tongue.
후에버 리북스 어 퍼선 윌 인 디 엔드 게인 페이버 래더 던 원 후 해즈 어 플래터링 텅.
사람을 경책하는 자는 혀로 아첨하는 자보다 나중에 더욱 사랑을 받느니라

24 Whoever robs their father or mother and says, "It's not wrong," is partner to one who destroys.
후에버 라브즈 데어 파더 오어 머더 언드 세즈, 잇스 낫 롱, 이즈 파아트너 투 원 후 디스트로이즈.
부모의 물건을 도둑질하고서도 죄가 아니라 하는 자는 멸망 받게 하는 자의 동류니라

25 The greedy stirs up conflict, but those who trust in the LORD will prosper.
더 그리디 스터즈 업 칸플릭트, 벗 도우즈 후 트러스트 인 더 로어드 윌 프라스퍼.
욕심이 많은 자는 다툼을 일으키나 여호와를 의지하는 자는 풍족하게 되느니라

26 Those who trust in themselves are fools, but those who walk in wisdom are kept safe.
도우즈 후 트러스트 인 뎀셀브즈 아아 풀즈, 벗 도우즈 후 웍 인 위즈덤 아아 켑트 세이프.
자기의 마음을 믿는 자는 미련한 자요 지혜롭게 행하는 자는 구원을 얻을 자니라

27 Those who give to the poor will lack nothing, but those who close their eyes to them receive many curses.
도우즈 후 기브 투 더 푸어 윌 랙 너씽, 벗 도우즈 후 클로우스 데어 아이즈 투 뎀 러시브 메니 커시즈.
가난한 자를 구제하는 자는 궁핍하지 아니하려니와 못 본 체하는 자에게는 저주가 크리라

28 When the wicked rise to power, people go into hiding; but when the wicked perish, the righteous thrive.
웬 더 위커드 라이즈 투 파워, 피펄 고우 인투 하이딩 벗 웬 더 위커드 페어리쉬, 더 라이처스 쓰라이브.
악인이 일어나면 사람이 숨고 그가 멸망하면 의인이 많아지느니라

bold [bould] a. 대담한
crop [krɑp] n. 수확
sake [seik] n. 위함, 이익
heed [hiːd] vt. 주의하다
resist [rizíst] vt. …에 저항하다

deaf [def] a. 귀머거리의
prayer [prɛər] n. 빌기, 기도
along [əlɔ́ːŋ] prep. …을 따라
into [íntu] prep. …안으로
delude [dilúːd] vt. 미혹시키다

confess [kənfés] vt. 고백하다
tremble [trémbəl] vi. 떨다
renounce [rináuns] vt. 포기하다
harden [hɑ́ːrdn] vt. 굳히다
roaring [rɔ́ːriŋ] n. 포효 소리, 고함

companion [kəmpǽnjən] n. 동료	triumph [tráiəmf] n. 승리	torment [tɔ́:rment] n. 고통, 고뇌
profit [prάfit] n. 이익, 수익	rise [raiz] vi. 일어서다	tyrannical [tirǽnikəl] a. 폭군의
amass [əmǽs] vt. 모으다	hiding [háidiŋ] n. 숨김, 은폐	stingy [stíŋi] a. 쏘는

29장 1 Whoever remains stiff-necked after many rebukes will suddenly be destroyed—without remedy.
후에버 리메인즈 스티프넥트 애프터 메니 리뷰스 윌 서더늘리 비 디스트로이드 위다우트 레머디.
자주 책망을 받으면서도 목이 곧은 사람은 갑자기 패망을 당하고 피하지 못하리라

2 When the righteous thrive, the people rejoice; when the wicked rule, the people groan.
웬 더 라이처스 쓰라이브, 더 피펄 리조이스 웬 더 위커드 룰, 더 피펄 그로운.
의인이 많아지면 백성이 즐거워하고 악인이 권세를 잡으면 백성이 탄식하느니라

3 A man who loves wisdom brings joy to his father, but a companion of prostitutes squanders his wealth.
어 맨 후 러브즈 위즈덤 브링즈 조이 투 히즈 파더, 벗 어 컴패년 어브 프라스터튯스 스콴더즈 히즈 웰쓰.
지혜를 사모하는 자는 아비를 즐겁게 하여도 창기와 사귀는 자는 재물을 잃느니라

4 By justice a king gives a country stability, but those who are greedy for bribes tear it down.
바이 저스터스 어 킹 기브즈 어 컨트리 스터빌리티, 벗 도우즈 후 아아 그리디 포어 브라이브즈 테어 잇 다운.
왕은 정의로 나라를 견고하게 하나 뇌물을 억지로 내게 하는 자는 나라를 멸망시키느니라

5 Those who flatter their neighbors are spreading nets for their feet.
도우즈 후 플래터 데어 네이버즈 아아 스프레딩 넷스 포어 데어 핏.
이웃에게 아첨하는 것은 그의 발 앞에 그물을 치는 것이니라

6 Evildoers are snared by their own sin, but the righteous shout for joy and are glad.
이벌두어즈 아아 스네어드 바이 데어 오운 신, 벗 더 라이처스 샤우트 포어 조이 언드 아아 글래드.
악인이 범죄하는 것은 스스로 올무가 되게 하는 것이나 의인은 노래하고 기뻐하느니라

7 The righteous care about justice for the poor, but the wicked have no such concern.
더 라이처스 케어 어바우트 저스터스 포어 더 푸어, 벗 더 위커드 해브 노우 서치 컨선.
의인은 가난한 자의 사정을 알아 주나 악인은 알아 줄 지식이 없느니라

8 Mockers stir up a city, but the wise turn away anger.
마커즈 스터 업 어 시티, 벗 더 와이즈 턴 어웨이 앵거.
거만한 자는 성읍을 요란하게 하여도 슬기로운 자는 노를 그치게 하느니라

9 If a wise person goes to court with a fool, the fool rages and scoffs, and there is no peace.
이프 어 와이즈 퍼선 고우즈 투 코어트 윋 어 풀, 더 풀 레이지즈 언드 스코프스, 언드 데어 이즈 노우 피스.
지혜로운 자와 미련한 자가 다투면 지혜로운 자가 노하든지 웃든지 그 다툼은 그침이 없느니라

10 The bloodthirsty hate a person of integrity and seek to kill the upright.
더 블러드써스티 헤이트 어 퍼선 어브 인테그러티 언드 식 투 킬 디 업라이트.
피 흘리기를 좋아하는 자는 온전한 자를 미워하고 정직한 자의 생명을 찾느니라

11 Fools give full vent to their rage, but the wise bring calm in the end.
풀즈 기브 풀 벤트 투 데어 레이지, 벗 더 와이즈 브링 캄 인 디 엔드.
어리석은 자는 자기의 노를 다 드러내어도 지혜로운 자는 그것을 억제하느니라

12 If a ruler listens to lies, all his officials become wicked.

이프 어 룰러 리선즈 투 라이즈, 올 히즈 어피셜즈 비컴 위커드.
관원이 거짓말을 들으면 그의 하인들은 다 악하게 되느니라

13 The poor and the oppressor have this in common: The LORD gives sight to the eyes of both.
더 푸어 언드 디 업레서 해브 디스 인 카먼 더 로어드 기브즈 사이트 투 디 아이즈 어브 보우쓰.
가난한 자와 포학한 자가 섞여 살거니와 여호와께서는 그 모두의 눈에 빛을 주시느니라

14 If a king judges the poor with fairness, his throne will be established forever.
이프 어 킹 저지즈 더 푸어 윋 페어너스, 히즈 쓰로운 윌 비 이스태블리쉬트 퍼레버.
왕이 가난한 자를 성실히 신원하면 그의 왕위가 영원히 견고하리라

15 A rod and a reprimand impart wisdom, but a child left undisciplined disgraces its mother.
어 라드 언드 어 렙러맨드 임파아트 위즈덤, 벗 어 차일드 레프트 언디시플린드 디스그레이시즈 잇스 머더.
채찍과 꾸지람이 지혜를 주거늘 임의로 행하게 버려 둔 자식은 어미를 욕되게 하느니라

16 When the wicked thrive, so does sin, but the righteous will see their downfall.
웬 더 위커드 쓰라이브, 소우 더즈 신, 벗 더 라이처스 윌 시 데어 다운폴.
악인이 많아지면 죄도 많아지나니 의인은 그들의 망함을 보리라

17 Discipline your children, and they will give you peace; they will bring you the delights you desire.
디서플린 요어 칠드런, 언드 데이 윌 기브 유 피스 데이 윌 브링 유 더 딜랏스 유 디자여.
네 자식을 징계하라 그리하면 그가 너를 평안하게 하겠고 또 네 마음에 기쁨을 주리라

18 Where there is no revelation, people cast off restraint; but blessed is the one who heeds wisdom's instruction.
웨어 데어 이즈 노우 레벌레이션, 피펄 캐스트 오프 리스트레인트 벗 블레스트 이즈 더 원 후 히즈 위즈덤즈 인스트럭션.
묵시가 없으면 백성이 방자히 행하거니와 율법을 지키는 자는 복이 있느니라

19 Servants cannot be corrected by mere words; though they understand, they will not respond.
서번트스 캐낫 비 커렉터드 바이 미어 워즈 도우 데이 언더스탠드, 데이 윌 낫 리스판드.
종은 말로만 하면 고치지 아니하나니 이는 그가 알고도 따르지 아니함이니라

20 Do you see someone who speaks in haste? There is more hope for a fool than for them.
두 유 시 서뭔 후 스픽스 인 헤이스트? 데어 이즈 모어 호웁 포어 어 풀 던 포어 뎀.
네가 말이 조급한 사람을 보느냐 그보다 미련한 자에게 오히려 희망이 있느니라

21 A servant pampered from youth will turn out to be insolent.
어 서번트 팸퍼드 프럼 유쓰 윌 턴 아웃 투 비 인설런트.
종을 어렸을 때부터 곱게 양육하면 그가 나중에는 자식인 체하리라

22 An angry person stirs up conflict, and a hot-tempered person commits many sins.
앤 앵그리 퍼선 스터즈 업 칸플릭트, 언드 어 핫템퍼드 퍼선 커밋스 메니 신즈.
노하는 자는 다툼을 일으키고 성내는 자는 범죄함이 많으니라

23 Pride brings a person low, but the lowly in spirit gain honor.
프라이드 브링즈 어 퍼선 로우, 벗 더 로울리 인 스피럿 게인 아너.
사람이 교만하면 낮아지게 되겠고 마음이 겸손하면 영예를 얻으리라

24 The accomplices of thieves are their own enemies; they are put under oath and dare not testify.

디 어캄플러서즈 어브 씨브즈 아아 데어 오운 에너미즈 데이 아아 풋 언더 오우쓰 언드 데어 낫 테스티파이.
도둑과 짝하는 자는 자기의 영혼을 미워하는 자라 그는 저주를 들어도 진술하지 아니하느니라

25 Fear of man will prove to be a snare, but whoever trusts in the LORD is kept safe.
피어 어브 맨 윌 프루브 투 비 어 스네어, 벗 후에버 트러스트스 인 더 로어드 이즈 켑트 세이프.
사람을 두려워하면 올무에 걸리게 되거니와 여호와를 의지하는 자는 안전하리라

26 Many seek an audience with a ruler, but it is from the LORD that one gets justice.
메니 식 앤 아디언스 윋 어 룰러, 벗 잇 이즈 프럼 더 로어드 댓 원 겟스 저스터스.
주권자에게 은혜를 구하는 자가 많으나 사람의 일의 작정은 여호와께로 말미암느니라

27 The righteous detest the dishonest; the wicked detest the upright.
더 라이처스 디테스트 더 디사너스트 더 위커드 디테스트 디 업라이트.
불의한 자는 의인에게 미움을 받고 바르게 행하는 자는 악인에게 미움을 받느니라

without [wiðáut] prep. …없이
thrive [θraiv] vi. 번창하다
prostitute [prάstətjù:t] n. 매춘부
squander [skwάndər] vt. 낭비하다
wealth [welθ] n. 부, 재산
country [kʌ́ntri] n. 나라, 국가
stability [stəbíləti] n. 안정, 안정성
greedy [grí:di] a. 욕심 많은
tear [tiər] n. 눈물
spread [spred] vt. 펴다, 펼치다
net [net] n. 그물
care [kεər] n. 걱정, 근심
such [sʌtʃ] a. 그러한
vent [vent] vt. 드러내다
anger [ǽŋgər] n. 노염, 성
many [méni] a. 많은, 다수의
kill [kil] vt. 죽이다, 살해하다
forever [fərévər] ad. 영구히
reprimand [réprəmæ̀nd] n. 견책
low [lou] a. 낮은
oath [ouθ] n. 맹세, 서약
thieve [θi:v] vt. 훔치다
audience [ɔ́:diəns] n. 청중, 관중
accomplice [əkάmplis] n. 공범자

30장 1 The sayings of Agur son of Jakeh—an inspired utterance. This man's utterance to Ithiel: "I am weary, God, but I can prevail.
더 세이잉즈 어브 어거 선 어브 잭 앤 인스파여드 어터런스. 디스 맨즈 어터런스 투 이씨얼 아이 앰 위리, 가드, 벗 아이 캔 프리베일
이 말씀은 야게의 아들 아굴의 잠언이니 그가 이디엘 곧 이디엘과 우갈에게 이른 것이니라

2 Surely I am only a brute, not a man; I do not have human understanding.
슈얼리 아이 앰 오운리 어 브룻, 낫 어 맨 아이 두 낫 해브 휴먼 언더스탠딩.
나는 다른 사람에게 비하면 짐승이라 내게는 사람의 총명이 있지 아니하니라

3 I have not learned wisdom, nor have I attained to the knowledge of the Holy One.
아이 해브 낫 런드 위즈덤, 노어 해브 아이 어테인드 투 더 날러지 어브 더 호울리 원.
나는 지혜를 배우지 못하였고 또 거룩하신 자를 아는 지식이 없거니와

4 Who has gone up to heaven and come down? Whose hands have gathered up the wind? Who has wrapped up the waters in a cloak? Who has established all the ends of the earth? What is his name, and what is the name of his son? Surely you know!
후 해즈 곤 업 투 헤번 언드 컴 다운? 후즈 핸즈 해브 개더드 업 더 윈드? 후 해즈 랩트 업 더 워터즈 인 어 클로욱? 후 해즈 이스태블리쉬트 올 디 엔즈 어브 디 어쓰? 웟 이즈 히즈 네임, 언드 웟 이즈 더 네임 어브 히즈 선? 슈얼리 유 노우!
하늘에 올라갔다가 내려온 자가 누구인지, 바람을 그 장중에 모은 자가 누구인지, 물을 옷에 싼 자가 누구인지, 땅의 모든 끝을 정한 자가 누구인지, 그의 이름이 무엇인지, 그의 아들의 이름이 무엇인지 너는 아느냐

5 "Every word of God is flawless; he is a shield to those who take refuge in him.
에브리 워드 어브 가드 이즈 플롤러스 히 이즈 어 쉴드 투 도우즈 후 테익 레퓨지 인 힘.
하나님의 말씀은 다 순전하며 하나님은 그를 의지하는 자의 방패시니라
6 Do not add to his words, or he will rebuke you and prove you a liar.
두 낫 애드 투 히즈 워즈, 오어 히 윌 리북 유 언드 프루브 유 어 라여.
너는 그의 말씀에 더하지 말라 그가 너를 책망하시겠고 너는 거짓말하는 자가 될까 두려우니라
7 "Two things I ask of you, LORD; do not refuse me before I die:
투 씽즈 아이 애스크 어브 유, 로어드 두 낫 리퓨즈 미 비포어 아이 다이
내가 두 가지 일을 주께 구하였사오니 내가 죽기 전에 내게 거절하지 마시옵소서
8 Keep falsehood and lies far from me; give me neither poverty nor riches, but give me only my daily bread.
킵 팰스후드 언드 라이즈 파아 프럼 미 기브 미 나이더 파버티 노어 리처즈, 벗 기브 미 오운리 마이 데일리 브레드.
곧 헛된 것과 거짓말을 내게서 멀리 하옵시며 나를 가난하게도 마옵시고 부하게도 마옵시고 오직 필요한 양식으로 나를 먹이시옵소서
9 Otherwise, I may have too much and disown you and say, 'Who is the LORD?' Or I may become poor and steal, and so dishonor the name of my God.
어더와이즈, 아이 메이 해브 투 머치 언드 디소운 유 언드 세이, 후 이즈 더 로어드? 오어 아이 메이 비컴 푸어 언드 스틸, 언드 소우 디사너 더 네임 어브 마이 가드.
혹 내가 배불러서 하나님을 모른다 여호와가 누구냐 할까 하오며 혹 내가 가난하여 도둑질하고 내 하나님의 이름을 욕되게 할까 두려워함이니이다
10 "Do not slander a servant to their master, or they will curse you, and you will pay for it.
두 낫 슬랜더 어 서번트 투 데어 매스터, 오어 데이 윌 커스 유, 언드 유 윌 페이 포어 잇.
너는 종을 그의 상전에게 비방하지 말라 그가 너를 저주하겠고 너는 죄책을 당할까 두려우니라
11 "There are those who curse their fathers and do not bless their mothers;
데어 아아 도우즈 후 커스 데어 파더즈 언드 두 낫 블레스 데어 머더즈
아비를 저주하며 어미를 축복하지 아니하는 무리가 있느니라
12 those who are pure in their own eyes and yet are not cleansed of their filth;
도우즈 후 아아 퓨 인 데어 오운 아이즈 언드 옛 아아 낫 클렌즈드 어브 데어 필쓰
스스로 깨끗한 자로 여기면서도 자기의 더러운 것을 씻지 아니하는 무리가 있느니라
13 those whose eyes are ever so haughty, whose glances are so disdainful;
도우즈 후즈 아이즈 아아 에버 소우 호티, 후즈 글랜시즈 아아 소우 디스데인펄
눈이 심히 높으며 눈꺼풀이 높이 들린 무리가 있느니라
14 those whose teeth are swords and whose jaws are set with knives to devour the poor from the earth and the needy from among mankind.
도우즈 후즈 티쓰 아아 소어즈 언드 후즈 조즈 아아 셋 윋 나이브즈 투 디바워 더 푸어 프럼 디 어쓰 언드 더 니디 프럼 어멍 맨카인드.
앞니는 장검 같고 어금니는 군도 같아서 가난한 자를 땅에서 삼키며 궁핍한 자를 사람 중에서 삼키는 무리가 있느

니라

15 "The leech has two daughters. 'Give! Give!' they cry. "There are three things that are never satisfied, four that never say, 'Enough!':

더 리치 해즈 투 도터즈. 기브! 기브! 데이 크라이. 데어 아아 쓰리 씽즈 댓 아아 네버 새터스파이드, 포어 댓 네버 세이, 이너프!

거머리에게는 두 딸이 있어 다오 다오 하느니라 족한 줄을 알지 못하여 족하다 하지 아니하는 것 서넛이 있나니

16 the grave, the barren womb, land, which is never satisfied with water, and fire, which never says, 'Enough!'

더 그레이브, 더 배런 웜, 랜드, 위치 이즈 네버 새터스파이드 윋 워터, 언드 파여, 위치 네버 세즈, 이너프!

곧 스올과 아이 배지 못하는 태와 물로 채울 수 없는 땅과 족하다 하지 아니하는 불이니라

17 "The eye that mocks a father, that scorns an aged mother, will be pecked out by the ravens of the valley, will be eaten by the vultures.

디 아이 댓 막스 어 파더, 댓 스콘즈 앤 에이지드 머더, 윌 비 펙트 아웃 바이 더 레이번즈 어브 더 밸리, 윌 비 이턴 바이 더 벌처즈.

아비를 조롱하며 어미 순종하기를 싫어하는 자의 눈은 골짜기의 까마귀에게 쪼이고 독수리 새끼에게 먹히리라

18."There are three things that are too amazing for me, four that I do not understand:

데어 아아 쓰리 씽즈 댓 아아 투 어메이징 포어 미, 포어 댓 아이 두 낫 언더스탠드

내가 심히 기이히 여기고도 깨닫지 못하는 것 서넛이 있나니

19 the way of an eagle in the sky, the way of a snake on a rock, the way of a ship on the high seas, and the way of a man with a young woman.

더 웨이 어브 앤 이걸 인 더 스카이, 더 웨이 어브 어 스네익 안 어 락, 더 웨이 어브 어 쉽 안 더 하이 시즈, 언드 더 웨이 어브 어 맨 윋 어 영 워먼.

곧 공중에 날아다니는 독수리의 자취와 반석 위로 기어 다니는 뱀의 자취와 바다로 지나다니는 배의 자취와 남자가 여자와 함께 한 자취며

20 "This is the way of an adulterous woman: She eats and wipes her mouth and says, 'I've done nothing wrong.'

디스 이즈 더 웨이 어브 앤 어덜터러스 워먼 쉬 잇스 언드 와입스 허 마우쓰 언드 세즈, 아이브 던 너씽 롱.

음녀의 자취도 그러하니라 그가 먹고 그의 입을 씻음 같이 말하기를 내가 악을 행하지 아니하였다 하느니라

21 "Under three things the earth trembles, under four it cannot bear up:

언더 쓰리 씽즈 디 어쓰 트렘벌즈, 언더 포어 잇 캐낫 베어 업

세상을 진동시키며 세상이 견딜 수 없게 하는 것 서넛이 있나니

22 a servant who becomes king, a godless fool who gets plenty to eat,

어 서번트 후 비컴즈 킹, 어 가들러스 풀 후 겟스 플렌티 투 잇,

곧 종이 임금된 것과 미련한 자가 음식으로 배부른 것과

23 a contemptible woman who gets married, and a servant who displaces her mistress.

어 컨템프터벌 워먼 후 겟스 메어리드, 언드 어 서번트 후 디스플레이시즈 허 미스트러스.

미움 받는 여자가 시집 간 것과 여종이 주모를 이은 것이니라

24 "Four things on earth are small, yet they are extremely wise:

포어 씽즈 안 어쓰 아아 스몰, 옛 데이 아아 익스트리믈리 와이즈
땅에 작고도 가장 지혜로운 것 넷이 있나니

25 Ants are creatures of little strength, yet they store up their food in the summer;
앤트스 아아 크리처즈 어브 리털 스트렝쓰, 옛 데이 스토어 업 데어 푸드 인 더 서머
곧 힘이 없는 종류로되 먹을 것을 여름에 준비하는 개미와

26 hyraxes are creatures of little power, yet they make their home in the crags;
하이랙서즈 아아 크리처즈 어브 리털 파워, 옛 데이 메익 데어 호움 인 더 크래그즈
약한 종류로되 집을 바위 사이에 짓는 사반과

27 locusts have no king, yet they advance together in ranks;
로우커스트스 해브 노우 킹, 옛 데이 어드밴스 터게더 인 랭크스
임금이 없으되 다 떼를 지어 나아가는 메뚜기와

28 a lizard can be caught with the hand, yet it is found in kings' palaces.
어 리저드 캔 비 쿳 윋 더 핸드, 옛 잇 이즈 파운드 인 킹즈 팰러시즈.
손에 잡힐 만하여도 왕궁에 있는 도마뱀이니라

29 "There are three things that are stately in their stride, four that move with stately bearing:
데어 아아 쓰리 씽즈 댓 아아 스테잇리 인 데어 스트라이드, 포어 댓 무브 윋 스테잇리 베링
잘 걸으며 위풍 있게 다니는 것 서넛이 있나니

30 a lion, mighty among beasts, who retreats before nothing;
어 라이언, 마이티 어멍 비스트스, 후 릿릿스 비포어 너씽
곧 짐승 중에 가장 강하여 아무 짐승 앞에서도 물러가지 아니하는 사자와

31 a strutting rooster, a he-goat, and a king secure against revolt.
어 스트러팅 루스터, 어 히고우트, 언드 어 킹 시큐 어겐스트 리보울트.
사냥개와 숫염소와 및 당할 수 없는 왕이니라

32 "If you play the fool and exalt yourself, or if you plan evil, clap your hand over your mouth!
이프 유 플레이 더 풀 언드 이그졸트 요어셀프, 오어 이프 유 플랜 이벌, 클랩 요어 핸드 오우버 요어 마우쓰!
만일 네가 미련하여 스스로 높은 체하였거나 혹 악한 일을 도모하였거든 네 손으로 입을 막으라

33 For as churning cream produces butter, and as twisting the nose produces blood, so stirring up anger produces strife."
포어 애즈 처닝 크림 프러두서즈 버터, 언드 애즈 트위스팅 더 노우즈 프러두서즈 블러드, 소우 스터링 업 앵거 프러두서즈 스트라이프.
대저 젖을 저으면 엉긴 젖이 되고 코를 비틀면 피가 나는 것 같이 노를 격동하면 다툼이 남이니라

inspiration [inspəréiʃən] n. 영감
utterance [ʌ́tərəns] n. 말함, 발언
weary [wíəri] a. 피로한
brute [bru:t] n. 짐승
learned [lə́:rnid] a. 학문이 있는
wrap [ræp] vt. 감싸다
cloak [klouk] n. 외투, 망토
ask [æsk] vt. 묻다
die [dai] vi. 죽다
falsehood [fɔ́:lshùd] n. 거짓말
daily [déili] a. 매일의, 일상의
bread [bred] n. 빵, 생계
father [fɑ́:ðər] n. 아버지, 부친
mother [mʌ́ðər] n. 어머니
filth [filθ] n. 오물, 불결물
disdainful [disdéinfəl] a. 경멸적인
enough [inʌ́f] a. 충분한
raven [réivən] n. 갈가마귀
vulture [vʌ́ltʃər] n. 독수리
mistress [místris] n. 여주인
extremely [ikstrí:mli] ad. 극단으로
crag [kræg] n. 험한 바위산
lizard [lízərd] n. 도마뱀
revolt [rivóult] n. 반란, 반역

31장 1 The sayings of King Lemuel—an inspired utterance his mother taught him.
더 세이잉즈 어브 킹 레물 앤 인스파여드 어터런스 히즈 머더 톳 힘.
르무엘 왕이 말씀한 바 곧 그의 어머니가 그를 훈계한 잠언이라

2 Listen, my son! Listen, son of my womb! Listen, my son, the answer to my prayers!
리선, 마이 선! 리선, 선 어브 마이 웜! 리선, 마이 선, 디 앤서 투 마이 프레어즈!
내 아들아 내가 무엇을 말하랴 내 태에서 난 아들아 내가 무엇을 말하랴 서원대로 얻은 아들아 내가 무엇을 말하랴

3 Do not spend your strength on women, your vigor on those who ruin kings.
두 낫 스펜드 요어 스트렝쓰 안 위먼, 요어 비거 안 도우즈 후 루언 킹즈.
네 힘을 여자들에게 쓰지 말며 왕들을 멸망시키는 일을 행하지 말지어다

4 It is not for kings, Lemuel—it is not for kings to drink wine, not for rulers to crave beer,
잇 이즈 낫 포어 킹즈, 레물 잇 이즈 낫 포어 킹즈 투 드링크 와인, 낫 포어 룰러즈 투 크레이브 비어.
르무엘아 포도주를 마시는 것이 왕들에게 마땅하지 아니하고 왕들에게 마땅하지 아니하며 독주를 찾는 것이 주권자들에게 마땅하지 않도다

5 lest they drink and forget what has been decreed, and deprive all the oppressed of their rights.
레스트 데이 드링크 언드 퍼겟 윗 해즈 빈 디크리드, 언드 딥라이브 올 디 업레스트 어브 데어 라잇스.
술을 마시다가 법을 잊어버리고 모든 곤고한 자들의 송사를 굽게 할까 두려우니라

6 Let beer be for those who are perishing, wine for those who are in anguish!
렛 비어 비 포어 도우즈 후 아아 페어리쉥, 와인 포어 도우즈 후 아아 인 앵귀쉬!
독주는 죽게 된 자에게, 포도주는 마음에 근심하는 자에게 줄지어다

7 Let them drink and forget their poverty and remember their misery no more.
렛 뎀 드링크 언드 퍼겟 데어 파버티 언드 리멤버 데어 미저리 노우 모어.
그는 마시고 자기의 빈궁한 것을 잊어버리겠고 다시 자기의 고통을 기억하지 아니하리라

8 Speak up for those who cannot speak for themselves, for the rights of all who are destitute.
스픽 업 포어 도우즈 후 캐낫 스픽 포어 뎀셀브즈, 포어 더 라잇스 어브 올 후 아아 데스터툿.
너는 말 못하는 자와 모든 고독한 자의 송사를 위하여 입을 열지니라

9 Speak up and judge fairly; defend the rights of the poor and needy.
스픽 업 언드 저지 페얼리 디펜드 더 라잇스 어브 더 푸어 언드 니디.
너는 입을 열어 공의로 재판하여 곤고한 자와 궁핍한 자를 신원할지니라

10 A wife of noble character who can find? She is worth far more than rubies.
어 와이프 어브 노우벌 케릭터 후 캔 파인드? 쉬 이즈 워쓰 파아 모어 던 루비즈.
누가 현숙한 여인을 찾아 얻겠느냐 그의 값은 진주보다 더 하니라

11 Her husband has full confidence in her and lacks nothing of value.
허 허즈번드 해즈 풀 칸퍼덴스 인 허 언드 랙스 너씽 어브 밸류.
그런 자의 남편의 마음은 그를 믿나니 산업이 핍절하지 아니하겠으며

12 She brings him good, not harm, all the days of her life.
쉬 브링즈 힘 구드, 낫 함, 올 더 데이즈 어브 허 라이프.
그런 자는 살아 있는 동안에 그의 남편에게 선을 행하고 악을 행하지 아니하느니라

13 She selects wool and flax and works with eager hands.
쉬 설렉트스 월 언드 플랙스 언드 웍스 윈 이거 핸즈.
그는 양털과 삼을 구하여 부지런히 손으로 일하며

14 She is like the merchant ships, bringing her food from afar.
쉬 이즈 라익 더 머천트 쉽스, 브링잉 허 푸드 프럼 어파아.
상인의 배와 같아서 먼 데서 양식을 가져 오며

15 She gets up while it is still night; she provides food for her family and portions for her female servants.
쉬 겟스 업 와일 잇 이즈 스틸 나이트 쉬 프러바이즈 푸드 포어 허 패멀리 언드 포어션즈 포어 허 피메일 서번트스.
밤이 새기 전에 일어나서 자기 집안 사람들에게 음식을 나누어 주며 여종들에게 일을 정하여 맡기며

16 She considers a field and buys it; out of her earnings she plants a vineyard.
쉬 컨시더즈 어 필드 언드 바이즈 잇 아웃 어브 허 어닝즈 쉬 플랜트스 어 비느여드.
밭을 살펴 보고 사며 자기의 손으로 번 것을 가지고 포도원을 일구며

17 She sets about her work vigorously; her arms are strong for her tasks.
쉬 셋스 어바우트 허 웍 비거러슬리 허 아아므즈 아아 스트롱 포어 허 태스크스.
힘 있게 허리를 묶으며 자기의 팔을 강하게 하며

18 She sees that her trading is profitable, and her lamp does not go out at night.
쉬 시즈 댓 허 트레이딩 이즈 프라퍼터벌, 언드 허 램프 더즈 낫 고우 아웃 앳 나이트.
자기의 장사가 잘 되는 줄을 깨닫고 밤에 등불을 끄지 아니하며

19 In her hand she holds the distaff and grasps the spindle with her fingers.
인 허 핸드 쉬 호울즈 더 디스태프 언드 그래스프스 더 스핀덜 윈 허 핑거즈.
손으로 솜뭉치를 들고 손가락으로 가락을 잡으며

20 She opens her arms to the poor and extends her hands to the needy.
쉬 오우펀즈 허 아아므즈 투 더 푸어 언드 익스텐즈 허 핸즈 투 더 니디.
그는 곤고한 자에게 손을 펴며 궁핍한 자를 위하여 손을 내밀며

21 When it snows, she has no fear for her household; for all of them are clothed in scarlet.
웬 잇 스노우즈, 쉬 해즈 노우 피어 포어 허 하우스호울드 포어 올 어브 뎀 아아 클로욷드 인 스카얼럿.
자기 집 사람들은 다 홍색 옷을 입었으므로 눈이 와도 그는 자기 집 사람들을 위하여 염려하지 아니하며

22 She makes coverings for her bed; she is clothed in fine linen and purple.
쉬 메익스 커버링즈 포어 허 베드 쉬 이즈 클로욷드 인 파인 리넌 언드 퍼펄.
그는 자기를 위하여 아름다운 이불을 지으며 세마포와 자색 옷을 입으며

23 Her husband is respected at the city gate, where he takes his seat among the elders of the land.
허 허즈번드 이즈 리스펙티드 앳 더 시티 게이트, 웨어 히 테익스 히즈 싯 어멍 디 엘더즈 어브 더 랜드.
그의 남편은 그 땅의 장로들과 함께 성문에 앉으며 사람들의 인정을 받으며

24 She makes linen garments and sells them, and supplies the merchants with sashes.
쉬 메익스 리넌 가아먼트스 언드 셀즈 뎀, 언드 서플라이즈 더 머천트스 윈 새쉬즈.
그는 베로 옷을 지어 팔며 띠를 만들어 상인들에게 맡기며

25 She is clothed with strength and dignity; she can laugh at the days to come.

쉬 이즈 클로욷드 윋 스트렝쓰 언드 디그너티 쉬 캔 래프 앳 더 데이즈 투 컴.
능력과 존귀로 옷을 삼고 후일을 웃으며

26 She speaks with wisdom, and faithful instruction is on her tongue.
쉬 스픽스 윋 위즈덤, 언드 페이쓰펄 인스트럭션 이즈 안 허 텅.
입을 열어 지혜를 베풀며 그의 혀로 인애의 법을 말하며

27 She watches over the affairs of her household and does not eat the bread of idleness.
쉬 와처즈 오우버 디 어페어즈 어브 허 하우스호울드 언드 더즈 낫 잇 더 브레드 어브 아이덜너스.
자기의 집안일을 보살피고 게을리 얻은 양식을 먹지 아니하나니

28 Her children arise and call her blessed; her husband also, and he praises her:
허 칠드런 어아이즈 언드 콜 허 블레스트 허 허즈번드 올소우, 언드 히 프레이지즈 허
그의 자식들은 일어나 감사하며 그의 남편은 칭찬하기를

29 "Many women do noble things, but you surpass them all."
메니 위먼 두 노우벌 씽즈, 벗 유 서패스 뎀 올.
덕행 있는 여자가 많으나 그대는 모든 여자보다 뛰어나다 하느니라

30 Charm is deceptive, and beauty is fleeting; but a woman who fears the LORD is to be praised.
참 이즈 디셉티브, 언드 뷰티 이즈 플리팅 벗 어 워먼 후 피어즈 더 로어드 이즈 투 비 프레이즈드.
고운 것도 거짓되고 아름다운 것도 헛되나 오직 여호와를 경외하는 여자는 칭찬을 받을 것이라

31 Honor her for all that her hands have done, and let her works bring her praise at the city gate.
아너 허 포어 올 댓 허 핸즈 해브 던, 언드 렛 허 웍스 브링 허 프레이즈 앳 더 시티 게이트.
그 손의 열매가 그에게로 돌아갈 것이요 그 행한 일로 말미암아 성문에서 칭찬을 받으리라

womb [wuːm] n. 자궁
spend [spend] vt. 쓰다, 소비하다
vigor [vígər] n. 활기, 정력
deprive [dipráiv] vt. 박탈하다
anguish [ǽŋgwiʃ] n. 고통, 괴로움
misery [mízəri] n. 불행, 고통
destitute [déstətjùːt] a. 빈곤한
defend [difénd] vt. 막다, 지키다
needy [níːdi] a. 가난한
harm [hɑːrm] n. 해, 위해
select [silékt] vt. 선택하다
wool [wul] n. 양털, 울
eager [íːgər] a. 열망하는
merchant [mə́ːrtʃənt] n. 상인
portion [pɔ́ːrʃən] n. 일부
task [tæsk] n. 일, 임무
distaff [dístæf] n. 실톳대
spindle [spíndl] n. 가락
elder [éldər] a. 손위의
scarlet [skɑ́ːrlit] n. 주홍, 진홍색
purple [pə́ːrpəl] a. 자줏빛의
affair [əfɛ́ər] n. 일, 용건
idleness [áidlnis] n. 나태
charm [tʃɑːrm] n. 매력

도서출판 사랑의장막 저서들

분별과 투시로 열리는 영적세계

저자 김다윗

우상 숭배와 음란으로 실패하는 삶의 원인을
규명해 주고 승리의 삶으로 이끌어주는 안내서이다.

14차원으로 열리는 성령의 세계 – 제1권 불의 4차원

저자 김다윗

하나님의 자녀로서 권세 있는 삶을 살아가는 비결은 오직 성령의
충만함에 있다. 이 책은 깊은 기도의 영성으로 열리는 성령의
3속성을 14단계로 풀어 쉽게 이해할 수 있도록 설명하고 있다.

사랑하는 사람들을 향한 사랑의 노래

저자 이해경

시집으로 자녀를 향한 사랑의 노래, 남편과 아내를 향한
사랑의 노래, 하나님을 향한 사랑의 노래, 비전을 향한
사랑의 노래가 수록되어 있다.

개역개정 지혜의 성경 잠언 따라쓰기

사랑의장막 편집부

잠언은 우리 자녀들을 명철하며, 지혜롭게,
공의롭게, 정의롭게, 정직하게 자라나게 합니다.

개역개정 약속의 성경 요절 따라쓰기

사랑의장막 편집부

성경은 하나님의 약속으로 가득합니다. 약속의 성경 요절따라쓰기는
우리 자녀들이 예수님을 믿는 믿음 안에서 천국에 대한 확실한 소망을
가지고 살아가기를 바라는 마음으로 만든 책입니다.

NIV개정 지혜의 성경 영어잠언 따라쓰기 1, 2 (전 2권)

사랑의장막 편집부

영어잠언 따라쓰기를 쓰면서 좋은 영어 글씨체를 갖게 되고,
원어민 발음과 한국어 성경(개역개정)을 수록하여 영어 잠언이 쉽게
읽어집니다. 또한 각 페이지마다 숙어와 예문, 각 장마다 단어를 정리하여
영어 해석에 도움이 됩니다.